SYLVIA

SYLVIA

a romantic comedy

by

A. R. Gurney

The Fireside Theatre

Garden City, NY

Photos of the 1995 Off Broadway production at the Manhattan Theatre Club by Joan Marcus.
Design by Maria Chiarino
ISBN: 1-56865-158-9

SYLVIA opened at New York's City Center Stage I on May 23, 1995 under the auspices of the Manhattan Theatre club: Lynne Meadow, Artistic Director and Barry Grove, Managing Director. It was directed by John Tillinger. The set was designed by John Lee Beatty, the costumes by Jane Greenwood, the lighting by Ken Billington and the sound by Aural Fixation. The production stage manager was Roy Harris. The cast was as follows:

SYLVIA . . . . Sarah Jessica Parker*
GREG . . . . Charles Kimbrough**
KATE . . . . Blythe Danner***
TOM, PHYLLIS and LESLIE . . . . Derek Smith

* The role was subsequently played by Jan Hooks.
** The role was subsequently played by John Cunningham.
*** The role was subsequently played by Mariette Hartley. Mariette Hartley was subsequently replaced by Mary Beth Peil.

CAST

SYLVIA

GREG

KATE

TOM, PHYLLIS and LESLIE to be played by one other actor

SET

A sense of the Manhattan skyline behind.

A Manhattan apartment, with a couch, a coffee table, a stuffed chair and a desk with a telephone and a desk chair.

Other areas as described; the simpler, the better. Elements of the basic apartment set may serve as components in subsequent scenes. The coffee table may become a park bench, for example. Kate's desk may also be Leslie's. The point is to keep the play flowing.

Props as needed.

To Sarah Jessica Parker
with love and amazement

Act
One

ACT I

BEFORE RISE: *Romantic music, evoking New York. A Benny Goodman Quartet, Gershwin or something else suggesting the city.*

AT RISE: *Greg and Kate's apartment. Sylvia comes on, followed by Greg, holding a leash and a newspaper. She is pert and sexy. Her hair is messy and she wears rather scruffy clothes: a baggy sweater, patched jeans, knee pads and old boots. A small nametag in the shape of a heart hangs around her neck. Greg wears business clothes, but his tie is loose. He watches Sylvia wander inquisitively around the room. She occasionally might take a sniff of something.*

GREG: What are you doing, Sylvia?

SYLVIA: Looking around.

GREG: Relax, why don't you?

SYLVIA: I gotta get used to things. (*She prowls again*)

GREG: Sit, Sylvia.

(*She tries kneeling, gets up immediately*)

SYLVIA: I'm not ready to sit.

GREG: I said, sit.

SYLVIA: I'm too nervous to sit.

GREG: Down, Sylvia. Down.

3

SYLVIA (*checking the couch*): I'm worried about where I sleep. Do I sleep on this couch?

GREG (*going to her*): I said sit DOWN, Sylvia. (*As she comes by, he gives her a gentle smack on the butt with his rolled-up newspaper*) SIT. DOWN.

SYLVIA: Ouch.

GREG: Then sit!

SYLVIA: I'm sitting, I'm sitting. (*She sits*)

GREG: Good girl. Now stay.

SYLVIA: I'm staying.

GREG (*patting her on the head*): Good girl. That's a very good girl. (*He goes to his chair, sits, starts to read the paper*)

SYLVIA: You don't have to hit, you know.

GREG: It didn't hurt.

SYLVIA: It most certainly did!

GREG: Then I'm sorry.

SYLVIA: You ought to be.

GREG: I just want you to be on your best behavior. Kate gets home any minute.

SYLVIA: Who's Kate?

GREG: My wife. O.K.?

SYLVIA: O.K. But you don't have to hit.

GREG: Then I won't. Ever again. I promise.

SYLVIA: O.K. (*He reads. Sylvia sits looking at him. Finally:*) I love you.

GREG: You do?

SYLVIA: I really do.

GREG: I think you do.

SYLVIA: Even when you hit me, I love you.

GREG: Thank you, Sylvia.

SYLVIA (*getting up*): I think you're God, if you want to know.

GREG: No, now sit.

SYLVIA: But I think you're God.

GREG: No, now stay, Sylvia. Stay. And sit.

SYLVIA: I want to sit near you.

GREG: Well, all right.

SYLVIA: Nearer, my God, to thee.

GREG: O.K. As long as you sit. (*Sylvia settles at his feet*) Good girl. Now let me read the paper. (*He reads. She looks at him adoringly for another long time*)

SYLVIA: You saved my life.

GREG: I guess I did.

SYLVIA: You did. You saved my goddamn *life*. I never would have survived out there on my own.

GREG: I did what anyone would do, Sylvia.

SYLVIA: Oh no. Someone else might have ignored me. Or shooed me away. Or even turned me in. Not you. You welcomed me with open arms. I really appreciate that.

GREG: Thanks, Sylvia.

SYLVIA: I hardly knew where to turn. I was beginning to panic. I thought my days were numbered. Then there you were.

GREG: There I was, all right.

SYLVIA: I felt some immediate connection. Didn't you?

GREG: I did, actually.

SYLVIA: I feel it now.

GREG: So do I. (*Puts down his paper; looks at her*) I do, Sylvia. (*He scratches her ears*) You're a good girl, Sylvia. I'll try to give you a good home.

SYLVIA: Thanks, Greg. And I'll try to show my appreciation. (*He returns to his paper. She sits staring at him adoringly, her chin on the arm of the chair. She sneezes. He smiles at her. Then suddenly she jumps to her feet*) Hey!

GREG: What's the matter?

SYLVIA (*looking off*):   Hey! Hey! Hey!

GREG: What? (*He listens*) Oh, that. That's the door. That's just Kate. Home from work.

SYLVIA: Hey! Hey!

GREG: Stop barking, Sylvia! She's a teacher. She likes an orderly classroom. Now show her you can be a good girl.

SYLVIA (*unable to control herself*):   Hey! Hey! Hey! Hey!

GREG: No, now quiet, Sylvia! Quiet down! Be a good, quiet girl.

KATE'S VOICE (*calling from off*):   Hello!

SYLVIA: Hey! Hey!

GREG: PLEASE, Sylvia. Please. Make a good first impression.

(*Kate comes on, brisk, well-dressed, carrying a large tote bag*)

KATE: Am I crazy? I thought I heard a—(*sees Sylvia*) Dog.

GREG: This is Sylvia, Kate.

SYLVIA (*approaching Kate*):   Hi.

GREG;   Sylvia, this is Kate.

KATE: What's going on, Greg?

SYLVIA (*walking around Kate, looking her over*):   Hi. I like you. I think I like you. Hi. (*Gives Kate a tentative kiss*)

KATE (*brushing her off*):   Stop that. Go away! (*To Greg*) Greg, what is this?

GREG: Now, Kate . . . sit, Sylvia.

SYLVIA: I was just trying to—

GREG: I said SIT.

(*Sylvia sits immediately*)

SYLVIA: See?

GREG: Good girl. (*To Kate*) Isn't she a good girl?

KATE: What's the story, Greg?

GREG: I found her in the park.

KATE: The park?

GREG: I was sitting in the park, and she jumped right into my lap.

KATE: Back up, please. You were *sitting?* In the *park?* When were you sitting in the park?

GREG: This afternoon. I took a break from the office. (*Pause*) I had another fight with Harold. (*Pause*) So I went to the park to cool off.

KATE: Oh, Greg.

GREG: I was just sitting there. And up came Sylvia.

SYLVIA (*going to him*): I love you.

GREG: I know you do, Sylvia. But sit.

SYLVIA (*sitting by him*): Gladly, Greg.

KATE: Tell me another, Greg.

GREG: It's true.

KATE: You called to her.

GREG: I did not.

KATE (*crossing to her desk*): You whistled. Beckoned. Something. You're always doing that with dogs.

GREG: I didn't this time, Kate. Actually I was asleep. I was dozing in the sun. And suddenly: Sylvia. Right, Sylvia?

SYLVIA: Right. Right. Exactly.

(*Pause. Kate looks at Sylvia*)

KATE: Sylvia?

GREG: Sylvia.

KATE: Why *Sylvia?*

GREG: The name was on her tag. (*Showing her*) See? "Sylvia."

KATE: What else is on her tag?

GREG: Nothing. Look. Just "Sylvia." She was lost and abandoned, Kate.

KATE (*skeptically*): Sylvia . . .

SYLVIA (*waving to her*): Hi, Kate.

GREG: See? She knows. She answers to it, don't you, Sylvia?

SYLVIA: I do! I definitely do!

KATE: What a name for a dog! Sylvia.

GREG: No, it fits. I looked it up. It means "She of the woods."

(*Sylvia is now scratching vigorously*)

KATE: She of the woods has fleas.

GREG: I'll deal with that. I'll get her all checked out.

KATE: Why, Greg?

GREG: To deal with the fleas.

KATE: No, I mean why a dog, darling?

GREG: Why not?

KATE: In the *city*, Greg?

GREG: I like dogs.

KATE: I know, sweetheart. But here? Now? With the kids gone?

GREG: I love dogs.

SYLVIA (*going to him*): I love *you*.

GREG: See? She knows that. She sensed it immediately. She latched right on.

KATE: I'm latching right off, Greg.

GREG: What do you mean?

KATE: Sweetheart, I'm exercising a veto. I'm saying no to Sylvia.

GREG: No?

KATE: N period. O period. Not in New York. Not at this stage of our lives. No.

GREG: Katie . . .

KATE: You work all day, *I* work all day. We go out a lot.

SYLVIA (*jumping up*):   "Out"? Did I hear "out"?

KATE: We're going out tonight, as a matter of fact.

SYLVIA: I love that word "out."

GREG: Tonight?

KATE: The Waldmans have tickets to a chamber music concert. So we're meeting for dinner, and going to that. Remember?

GREG: Oh, right.

KATE: And tomorrow night we have our Spanish lessons, and Saturday we're going to the Knicks game with the Kramers . . . so no, Greg. No Sylvia. There's no need.

GREG: *I* have a need.

KATE: What need?

GREG: I'm not sure. But I have it.

KATE: Oh, Greg.

GREG: It's a definite need.

KATE: Oh, Greg.

GREG: If I could ex*plain* it, Kate, if I could put it neatly into words, then it wouldn't be so much of a need.

SYLVIA: I love you, Greg.

GREG: And she needs me.

SYLVIA: When do we eat?

KATE: She needs anyone who'll give her a meal.

GREG: No, it's more than that. Much more. We've bonded, Kate.

KATE: Ooo. Ouch. That's an overworked word, Greg.

GREG: I really want her, Kate.

KATE: And I really don't. So what do we do?

GREG: I don't know.

SYLVIA (*to herself*):   I hate situations like this. I've been caught in the middle before, and I just hate it.

KATE (*looking at Sylvia*):   What is she? A mutt?

GREG: I think she's part Lab.

KATE: She's a mutt.

GREG: She's got a Lab's disposition. She likes everybody, don't you, Sylvia?

SYLVIA: I do. Everybody. My aim in life is to please.

GREG: I also think she may be part poodle.

SYLVIA (*assuming a saucy position*): *Mais oui, Monsieur. Ooo la la.*

KATE: She's not the most beautiful thing I've ever seen, Greg. (*She goes out*)

GREG (*calling after her*): That's what I like about her. (*To Sylvia*) You've got hybrid vigor, don't you, Sylvia? You are multicultural.

SYLVIA: You better believe it.

GREG (*calling to Kate*): Think of her as an American, Kate! (*To Sylvia*) Canus Americanus, that's Sylvia.

SYLVIA: I pledge allegiance. (*Brooklyn accent*) I solemnly swear.

KATE'S VOICE (*from within*): Is she housetrained?

GREG: I think so.

KATE'S VOICE: You *think* so?

GREG: Are you housetrained, Sylvia?

SYLVIA (*uneasily*):   Oh, yes. Definitely. Absolutely.
No question.

KATE'S VOICE: She probably isn't.

GREG: She was a good girl walking home, weren't
you, Sylvia? You were a very good girl.

SYLVIA (*rolling around*):   Yes, I was. I was very good.

GREG: We were a very good girl. Twice. Weren't
we?

(*Kate returns with two drinks, sees this display*)

KATE: I may puke, Greg.

GREG: Oh, look, sweetheart. Give her a chance.
Poor lost soul.

KATE: Seems to me someone else around here is
behaving like a poor lost soul.

GREG: All the more reason, sweetheart. Maybe
that's the need.

(*The telephone rings*)

KATE: I'll get it. (*She answers*) Oh, yes, Harold.
He's right here. (*Hands over receiver*) He wants to
talk.

GREG: I don't feel like talking.

KATE: He's your *boss,* for God's sake!

GREG: I'll take it in the other room. (*Starts off*)

KATE: He sounded a little mad, Greg.

GREG: Yes, well, I'm mad, too. The guy thinks he owns me.

KATE: I hope you apologize.

GREG: For what?

KATE: For leaving work! In the middle of the day!

GREG: It's the best thing I've done in years.

KATE: Oh, yes? Why?

GREG: It got me Sylvia.

KATE: Oh, come on!

(*He goes; Kate goes to her desk. She and Sylvia eye each other*)

SYLVIA (*finally*):   Hi. (*Kate sits at her desk, takes books and a notebook out of her bag, begins to work*) I said hi.

KATE (*working*):   I'm busy, Sylvia.

(*Sylvia goes to her, nudges her*)

SYLVIA: Hello, Kate.

KATE: Go away, Sylvia.

SYLVIA: I'm just trying to make friends.

KATE: Don't bother me, please. I'm trying to prepare my fall curriculum.

SYLVIA: You don't like me, do you?

KATE (*working*):   It's not a question of that.

SYLVIA: You don't like dogs.

KATE: I like them when they belong to other people.

SYLVIA: You're prejudiced.

KATE: Not at all.

SYLVIA: I think you're prejudiced against dogs!

KATE (*putting down her work*):   I am not prejudiced, Sylvia. When I was a girl, I read the Albert Payson Terhune dog books cover to cover. I watched *Lassie* on television. I'm a huge fan of *One Hundred and One Dalmatians*. When we lived in the suburbs, when the children were around, we had several dogs, and guess who ended up feeding the damn things. But I don't want a dog *now*, Sylvia. That is the point. Our last child has gone off to college, and we have moved into town and the dog phase of my life is definitely over. I've gotten my Master's degree, Sylvia, and I have a very challenging teaching job, and frankly I don't want to worry about animals. So if you'll excuse me, I will return to the daunting task of planning how to teach Shakespeare in the inner city junior high school. (*She returns to her work*)

SYLVIA: O.K. Fine. No problem. (*She goes to the couch*) I'll just stay out of your hair. (*She steps onto the couch, turns around once or twice, then settles on it*)

KATE (*looking up*):   Off, Sylvia!

SYLVIA: You speaking to me?

KATE: I said off that couch! Right now!

SYLVIA: I'm just relaxing. Can't I even relax?

(*Kate leaves her desk, pulls Sylvia off the couch*)

KATE: Now off! And stay off!

SYLVIA: Easy! Take it easy! . . . Jesus!

KATE: I'm sorry, but you've got to learn. (*She returns to her work. Pause*)

SYLVIA (*sitting grumpily on the floor*):   I've sat on couches before, you know.

KATE (*working*):   What?

SYLVIA: I said I've sat on couches before. I've sat on plenty of couches.

KATE: Well, you can't sit on this one.

SYLVIA: Hoity-toity to you.

KATE: Quiet. I'm working.

SYLVIA (*getting up; easing onto the chair*): Can I at least sit on a chair?

KATE: No, Sylvia. Off!

SYLVIA (*slumping again onto the floor*): Shit. Piss. Fuck.

KATE (*putting down her pencil*): This is not going to work, Sylvia.

SYLVIA: What do you mean?

KATE: I'm afraid you'll have to go to the pound.

SYLVIA: Hey, I'm sitting, aren't I? I'm sitting on the floor. Look how quickly I sat.

KATE: Still, you've got to go.

SYLVIA: O.K. I get the picture. I'll avoid the furniture. I'm not dumb.

KATE: No, I'm sorry, Sylvia. You're going to the pound. I'm sure someone will come along and give you a nice home.

SYLVIA: I've got a nice home right here.

KATE: No, now listen, Sylvia. It doesn't make sense. Nobody's around all day long. You'd be bored out of your mind, stuck in this apartment.

SYLVIA: I don't mind. I'll sleep. I'll chew things.

KATE: That's just the trouble.

SYLVIA: All right. I *won't* chew things. Just show me the rules and I'll follow them, I swear.

KATE: We go out a lot, Sylvia. We visit friends in the country on weekends. We see the kids at college.

SYLVIA: I'll come, too!

KATE (*crossing to her*):   No, I don't want that. I want my freedom, Sylvia. I want freedom from dogs. Now, you'll be much happier somewhere else.

SYLVIA: In the *pound?*

KATE: Well, not the *pound*, really, Sylvia. I shouldn't have said the pound. We'll give you to . . . what is it? The Animal Rescue League. Or the Humane Society.

SYLVIA: They suck.

KATE: Now, now.

SYLVIA: They *suck!* You have no idea what they do.

KATE: Well, I'm sure they make every effort to—

SYLVIA: Have you ever been there? Have you ever bothered to check them out?

KATE: No, but—

SYLVIA: The rows of cages. The shitty food.

KATE: Oh, now.

SYLVIA: The time limit.

KATE: The time limit?

SYLVIA: They all have time limits. They don't broadcast it, but they do. If someone doesn't bail you out, normally within five working days, then they put you to sleep.

KATE: Sylvia . . .

SYLVIA: They do! They kill you! Listen. It's a tough world out there, lady. I know. I've been there. (*Nuzzling her*) That's why I want to be here.

KATE: Well, you can't, Sylvia. I'm terribly sorry, but I really have to put my foot down.

(*Greg comes back in*)

GREG: Hey, Sylvia, baby!

SYLVIA (*going to him, kissing him*):   I love you! I love you!

KATE: Did you make it up with Harold?

GREG: We agreed to disagree.

KATE: Oh, Greg.

GREG: He keeps wanting to shift me into the money market.

KATE: What's wrong with that?

GREG: I'll tell you what's wrong with that. It's too abstract, that's what's wrong with that.

KATE: I don't see why.

GREG: Look, Kate. I liked manufacturing—starting off in product development. I liked that. I could see what we were making, I could touch it, I could tinker. And I liked selling, too, when they bumped me up to sales. I still knew the product. I could picture it in my mind. O.K. So then they acquire an investment company and tell me to trade. I try. I study up. I learn about oil, soybeans, corn. I read the forecasts, I figure the trends. I trade. And I do O.K. Not great, but I get by. But now they want me to trade currencies, Kate. Money markets. Derivatives. I can't do that, sweetheart. What's behind currencies? Other currencies. What's behind them? Who knows? Nothing to touch, to see, to get a purchase on. And that's what I mean when I say it's too abstract.

KATE: Don't lose your job, Greg.

GREG: It wouldn't kill me.

KATE: The kids would have to quit school!

GREG: That wouldn't kill *them*.

KATE: Oh, Greg.

GREG: I'm not so sure college is the answer to everything in life.

KATE: *You* went to college.

GREG: That's why I'm not so sure.

KATE: Oh, for God's sake . . .

GREG: If they really want college, they'll find ways of paying for it. They might get more out of it, too.

KATE: I can't believe I'm hearing this!

GREG: Neither can I. That's what makes it so exciting. (*He waves furtively to Sylvia*)

KATE: So how did you leave it with Harold, Greg?

GREG: I told him to put me in something real.

KATE: Real? What's real?

GREG: Sylvia's real, aren't you, Sylvia?

SYLVIA (*leaping into his arms*):   I sure try to be!

KATE: Down, Sylvia! . . . make her get down, Greg!

GREG (*gently letting Sylvia down*):   Down, Sylvia.

KATE: She'll ruin your clothes.

GREG: Don't jump up, Sylvia.

SYLVIA: Sorry. I went a little overboard there.

GREG: Let me at least try her, Kate.

KATE: For how long?

GREG: A few days, at least.

KATE: All right. For a few days.

SYLVIA: Yippee! Yay! I sense a change in the weather here.

KATE: For a few days we will *try* Sylvia. In the fervent hope that you'll realize how dumb it is to take on a dog at this point in our lives.

GREG: Fair enough, Kate.

SYLVIA (*standing by Greg*): You're happy, I'm happy.

KATE: No, now wait. I also want one thing clear, Greg: she's yours, not mine. I won't feed her, and I won't walk her, and I don't want her jumping onto any of the—(*sees something on the floor*) What's that?

GREG: What's what?

KATE: That puddle. She's peed, Greg.

GREG: Did you do that, Sylvia?

SYLVIA: I won't dignify that with an answer.

KATE: Of course she did that.

SYLVIA: I'm not saying a word.

GREG: She was nervous, Kate. Strange place. Hostile atmosphere . . .

SYLVIA: That's it. That was the problem.

KATE: You should punish her, Greg!

GREG: I can't punish her, it's too late to punish her.

SYLVIA (*hugging him*):   I love this man. I adore him.

KATE: Rub her nose in it at least! She's got to learn!

GREG: I won't do that, Kate!

SYLVIA: Hey! Hey! Hey!

KATE: Quiet, you!

SYLVIA: I'm getting nervous. I might bite.

GREG: No, now relax, Sylvia.

KATE: At least clean it up, Greg.

GREG: Glad to. (*He uses his newspaper*)

SYLVIA (*watching him*):   This is slightly embarrassing.

KATE: Honestly! Springing a dog on me this way!

GREG: There! All cleaned up! See? Not a trace!

SYLVIA: Wasn't there, didn't happen.

KATE: You've really thrown me a curve here, Greg.

GREG: Tell you what: we'll go out.

KATE: Out? Now?

SYLVIA: Did I hear the word "out"?

GREG (*to Kate*):   I meant Sylvia.

KATE: Oh.

GREG (*to Sylvia*):   Let's go out, Sylvia.

SYLVIA (*leaping into his arms again*):   Knew it! Can't wait! Love going out!

GREG: Down, Sylvia! Down!

SYLVIA (*getting down*):   But it's my favorite thing!

KATE (*exiting to get cleaning equipment*): What about the Waldmans?

SYLVIA (*finding her leash, handing it to him*): Let's go, Greg.

GREG (*calling toward off*): The Waldmans?

KATE'S VOICE: Dinner! The concert!

SYLVIA (*dragging him towards the front hall*): Come on, Greg!

GREG (*calling to Kate*): Take Betsy in my place. She loves concerts.

KATE (*returning with a spray cleaner and a cloth*): Sweetheart—

GREG (*as he is pulled by Sylvia*): Sylvia needs to go!

KATE: I'm worried, Greg. I'm worried about your job, I'm worried about you, I'm worried about us.

GREG (*as he is dragged off by Sylvia*): I'm worried about Sylvia at the moment.

KATE (*standing watching them*): "I must be cruel, only to be kind. (*She kneels to clean up the spot*) Thus bad begins . . . (*She sprays the "spot"*) . . . and worse remains behind." *Hamlet,* Act Three.

(MUSIC: *Nature music, such as Wagner's* Siegfried Idyll. *Kate goes off as the set changes to greenery. Bird sounds.*

Occasional sounds of dogs barking offstage. Greg and Sylvia come on, each holding an end of the leash)

GREG: Here we are, Sylvia. The park. Where we met. Remember?

SYLVIA: I'm nervous.

GREG: No. Hey, you're in your element now. This is nature, Sylvia. This is your natural habitat.

SYLVIA: I'm still nervous.

GREG: Look at those other dogs.

SYLVIA: I see them, I see them.

GREG: This is called Dog Hill. They allow dogs to play freely here. (*He takes the leash from her*) Go play, Sylvia. (*Giving her a shove*)

SYLVIA: Hey! Stop pushing.

GREG: Then go, Sylvia. There's your group, there's your pack. Call of the wild, kid.

SYLVIA: I know all that.

GREG: And you need the exercise.

SYLVIA: Look, it's no easy thing wading into a new group. They can gang up. Or bite. Or simply ignore you. I notice you're not barging into that group of dog owners.

GREG: You have a point.

SYLVIA: So. Let me take my own sweet time. (*She starts tentatively offstage*)

GREG (*watching her go*):   Good girl. (*Continuing to watch*) Good . . . go   on . . . play . . . run around . . . good.

(*Sylvia goes off. Tom comes on. He wears jeans, a windbreaker and a baseball cap*)

TOM: Hiya.

GREG: Hello.

TOM: New around here?

GREG: Just got a dog.

TOM: That one yours?

GREG: Right.

TOM: Cute.

GREG: Thanks.

TOM: Cute little butt on her.

GREG: I agree.

TOM: That's my Golden sniffing around her.

GREG: Good-looking dog.

TOM: His name's Bowser.

GREG: He looks like a Bowser.

TOM: He is. He is definitely a Bowser.

GREG: Mine's called Sylvia.

TOM: Sylvia? . . . Uh oh.

GREG: You don't like the name Sylvia?

TOM: Might cause problems.

GREG: Why?

TOM: Give a dog a woman's name, you begin to think of her as a woman.

GREG: Oh yes?

TOM: That can be dangerous. Which is why I go for doggy names. Spot. Fido. Bowser. . . . Sylvia? That can spell trouble.

GREG: Oh, come on.

TOM: Maybe I'm just associating. I had a girl named Sylvia.

GREG: Was she good-looking?

TOM: No, she was a dog.

(*Both laugh; then both watch*)

GREG: They seem to be getting along.

TOM: Sylvia and Bowser. (*Calling out*) Easy, Bowser. Go slow. (*To Greg*) Is Sylvia spayed?

GREG: She's a stray. I haven't had her checked yet.

TOM: Don't let them spay her till you're sure she's been in heat.

GREG: Don't?

TOM: It's a feminist thing. You're supposed to let her experience how it feels to be female. That way, she'll retain a sense of gender later on.

GREG: Ah.

TOM: There's a book on the subject. Called *Play Now, Spay Later*. I'll bring it the next time I come to the park.

GREG: Thanks.

(*Sylvia runs back on enthusiastically*)

SYLVIA: Just touching base here, just touching base.

GREG: Having a good time, Sylvia?

SYLVIA: The best!

GREG: Do you like Bowser?

SYLVIA: I think he's absolutely fantastic!

GREG: Then go back and play!

SYLVIA: May I?

GREG: Sure, kid! Go on! Shoo!

SYLVIA: Oh, boy! Look out, Bowser! Here I come!
(*She runs off*)

TOM: She's a little insecure, isn't she?

GREG: Why do you say that?

TOM: The way she checks back with you.

GREG: She loves me.

TOM: Ah.

GREG: She thinks I saved her life. I'm her knight
in shining armor.

TOM: Uh-oh.

GREG: Now what's the matter?

TOM: You married?

GREG: Sure. Why?

TOM: Wife fond of Sylvia?

GREG: Not yet. Why?

TOM: Kids out of the nest?

GREG: Right. Why?

TOM: Be careful.

GREG: What do you mean?

TOM: You can get lost in it.

GREG: Oh yes?

TOM: Sure. A man and his dog. It's a big thing.

GREG: I guess it is.

TOM: Women sense it. They nose it out. My wife feels very threatened by it.

GREG: She does?

TOM: Oh, God, yes. And I imagine it's worse with yours.

GREG: Why?

TOM: No offense, but you're older. With older guys, it can become major.

GREG: Think so?

TOM: Oh sure. It's something to hold on to, on the way down.

GREG: Oh now.

TOM: Look, women with dogs, no problem. A dog is basically another kid to them. It's a maternal thing. But for guys, it's different. When I come home at night, I have to *remind* myself to kiss my wife before I say hello to Bowser.

GREG: Mmm hmm.

TOM: I even think about him at work. I keep wanting to call him up and chew the fat. I don't think it's a gay thing, but I love that guy.

GREG: I can understand that.

TOM: And they say it's even worse if your dog's a female.

GREG: Really.

TOM: There was a guy here, had a dog named Debbie—half Bassett, half Beagle—sweet little thing. His wife walked in on him giving Debbie a bath and got so jealous she gave the dog away.

GREG: Christ! What did the guy do?

TOM: Sued her for damages. The judge was a dog owner and came down on his side. He said a man and his dog is a sacred relationship. What nature hath put together let no woman put asunder.

GREG: So what happened?

TOM: Well, the guy got Debbie back, and his wife back, and they all tried moving to Vermont. But it's still not good. Someone visited them recently and said it reminded him of the last chapter of *Ethan Frome*.

GREG: Good Lord.

TOM: There's a book out on the problem, actually. *Your Pooch and Your Partner*. It has one basic bit of advice. Always remember that your dog is simply a dog. Always keep reminding yourself of that fact. Not a person. Just a dog. Force yourself to think it. Otherwise you can get into deep dog-shit.

GREG: Gotcha.

TOM: Well. Time to go. Better hold Sylvia so she won't follow Bowser.

GREG: Oh, she won't do that.

TOM: She might. Bowser brings out the beast in them.

(*He goes off.* MUSIC: *something cozy and domestic, like "My Blue Heaven." Greg strolls off as the set becomes the apartment and Kate enters, settling at her desk*)

GREG'S VOICE: We're home!

KATE: Love that "we."

GREG (*coming on; he wears a different more informal shirt*):   Well, we are.

KATE: You're late again.

GREG: I lost track of the time.

KATE: This is the third time this week.

GREG (*kissing her*):   Time is for slaves, Katie.

KATE: Time is for people who have things to do. I have an evening meeting.

GREG: In the middle of August?

KATE: They're deciding to try a pilot program for my new English curriculum.

GREG (*kissing her*):   What? Hey! Congratulations! You're turning into a big cheese!

KATE: I try.

GREG: You do more than try! You succeed, baby!

KATE: Let's hope. (*She gathers up her books and papers*) Anyway, I had to eat early. The microwave stands waiting.

GREG: Fine.

KATE: Where's Saliva?

GREG: Her name is Sylvia, Kate.

KATE: Where is she?

GREG: She's a little hyper at the moment. I put her in the other room.

KATE: No wonder things seemed so peaceful.

GREG: Katie. Before you go, I've got a surprise for you.

KATE: A surprise?

GREG (*taking her to the chair, sitting her down*): Remember I said Sylvia was a little hyper?

KATE: I vaguely recall that observation, yes.

GREG: I'll show you why. (*He goes off*)

KATE (*checking her watch; calling off*): I haven't got much time, Greg.

(*Greg comes back on*)

GREG: Ta da. (*Calling off*) Sylvia: come. (*Proudly*) I had her professionally groomed.

(*Lush advertising music. Pink light. Sylvia comes on with a new hairdo, a bow in her hair and a corny outfit*)

SYLVIA: Look at me! Look at me! (*Shimmying*) How do you like them apples?

GREG: See why I was late? They gave her the full treatment: flea dip, nails clipped, ears cleaned, the works.

KATE (*dryly*): Really?

GREG: They even evacuated her anal glands.

KATE: Spare me, Greg.

GREG: O.K. But the girl who gave her the bath said she thought she was basically French poodle.

SYLVIA (*leaning against the arm of the couch, singing "La Vie en Rose" à la Dietrich*): *"Quand il me prend dans les bras . . ."*

GREG: They told me she was crawling with fleas. You were right about that, Katie. But now look at her. Isn't she spectacular?

SYLVIA (*singing à la Shirley Temple*): *"Darling, je vous aime beaucoup . . . Je ne sais pas* what to do." (*She jumps onto the couch*)

GREG: Don't you want to keep her now?

KATE: Off, Sylvia!

(*Sylvia burrows her nose into the couch*)

GREG: Oh, come on.

KATE: Off that couch, Sylvia! I don't want her on the furniture, Greg . . . OFF, Sylvia!

SYLVIA (*getting off the couch; throwing down the bow in her hair*): Well. I tried.

Sarah Jessica Parker as Sylvia.

All photos of the Manhattan Theatre Club's 1995 Off Broadway production by Joan Marcus.

Charles Kimbrough as Greg *(left)* with Sarah Jessica Parker as Sylvia.

Blythe Danner as Kate *(right)* with Sarah Jessica Parker as Sylvia.

Derek Smith as Phyllis *(right)* with Blythe Danner as Kate.

GREG (*bringing Sylvia to Kate*):   Smell her, Kate.

KATE: I don't want to smell her, Greg.

GREG: No, really. She smells great. Come on. Smell.

KATE: I can smell her from here, sweetie.

GREG: Then don't you think she smells great?

KATE: She smells like a lavatory in an airplane, Greg.

GREG: Oh, Kate.

KATE: All right. A lavatory in First Class.

GREG: At least you admit she's a class act.

SYLVIA (*holding out her hand to be kissed*):   *Enchantée, Madame.*

KATE (*rejecting the hand*):   I've really got to go.

GREG (*holding Sylvia up by her arms*):   But just *look* at her. Isn't she fucking gorgeous?

KATE: Greg, *don't* use that word, please, if you can possibly help it! I am spending my days trying to teach urban children the liberating possibilities of William Shakespeare in all his majesty and variety! I'd prefer not to come home to four-letter words! (*She goes out*)

SYLVIA (*looking after her*):   Dig *her*.

GREG: She's tired. She works hard.

SYLVIA: She doesn't like me.

GREG: She will, Sylvia.

SYLVIA: She makes me nervous. I sense the clock ticking away.

GREG: She just takes her time about things. Hey, it took her two years to say she'd marry me.

SYLVIA: Two *years?* Jesus, Greg! If you multiply that by seven why that's . . . um . . . carry the two . . . I make that fourteen years, dog time! That's too long, Greg!

GREG: She's worth it, Sylvia. I promise.

SYLVIA: Yeah, but can't I do something to speed things up, Greg? I'm tired of being just a houseguest around here. I want to feel totally at home. (*She puts a tentative foot on the couch*)

GREG: She'll come around. She's just a little ca-reer-oriented at the moment. It's a phase women are going through these days. . . . Come on. Let's see what there is for chow.

(*They go off, as we hear a telephone ringing. It is night. Kate comes on, wearing a bathrobe and carrying a porta-ble phone*)

KATE: Hello? . . . Oh hello, Harold. No, it's never too late, Harold . . . no, he's fine. Why did you think he was sick? . . . What? The whole afternoon? . . . I didn't know that, Harold, no . . . yes, well he's not here, Harold . . . he's out with the d-d-d—with a client, actually, Harold. Which, come to think of it, was where he was this afternoon. . . . Is it that late? Well, that must be because this client is a real party-animal . . . Yes, I'll tell Greg to stop by your office first thing. . . . Good night, Harold . . . (*She hangs up; to herself*) "Lord, Lord, how this world is given to lying." *Henry the Fourth, Part one.*

(*She goes off as we hear urban and moody music. Urban setting, late at night. Greg and Sylvia come on, holding either end of the leash*)

GREG: Know something? I'm beginning to like these late-night walks, Sylvia. . . . They're turning into a whole new thing.

SYLVIA: Excuse me? I was concentrating on that Doberman across the street.

GREG: I was just saying that these walks at night are giving me a whole new perspective on life. The city seems to be shaking itself down to its essentials. That truck delivering tomorrow's vegetables. That doorman keeping watch over his flock by night. That young couple, hurrying home to screw. Food, shelter, sex. The basic things stand out at night, Sylvia.

SYLVIA: Now wait. Go slow here. I'm not quite with you, Greg.

GREG: Remember when we passed that poor homeless woman huddled in the doorway? Or that scruffy guy poking in the garbage for soft-drink cans? Remember how I made eye contact with them, Sylvia? We recognized each other in ways we could never do during the day.

SYLVIA: Want to run that by me one more time?

GREG: I just mean that when I'm out here at night with you, all the bustle of the daytime world seems like an old game of Trivial Pursuits. (*By now Sylvia's leash is tangled around her feet*) I feel connected to my fellow creatures in a new and special way, Sylvia. (*He untangles her*) I feel part of some larger pack. Surely you can understand that.

SYLVIA: Nope. Thought I had it, but it slipped away.

GREG: Maybe it's just the anxieties of middle age. Or the sense of disillusionment which goes with late twentieth-century capitalism. I mean, the Cold War's over, Sylvia. We've won. But what have we got?

SYLVIA: I wish I could contribute something here, but I just plain can't. (*She sits*)

GREG: Never mind. Look, Sylvia! Look up there! Through all this urban haze, you can still see a

star! How long has it been since we've really
looked at the stars? Our early ancestors knew
them cold, Sylvia. They could read them like
books. (*Sylvia yawns*) They used them to guide
their way through forests and across deserts and
over the vast expanses of the sea. Birds and animals know them too, I hear. Migrating geese,
salmon, wildebeest . . .

SYLVIA: Huh?

GREG: I guess what I'm talking about is instinct,
Sylvia. Maybe we have instincts we don't even
know about. Maybe we are experiencing basic
pulls we don't even recognize. Maybe that vast
book of nature spread open above us is trying to
tell us things we once knew and have forgotten
and need to know again.

SYLVIA: Wow, Greg. Boy. Hmmm.

GREG: All I know is you trigger those instincts in
me, Sylvia. You take me back in some basic way.
Oh and hey, look! There's the moon! Catch that
moon, Sylvia, rising between those buildings!
How many people these days really notice the
moon?

SYLVIA: I suppose you'd like me to sit down and
howl at it.

GREG: I wouldn't mind.

SYLVIA: Well, I don't think I can do that, Greg.
Sorry. I like to think I've grown beyond that

kind of behavior. (*She sniffs something*) Excuse me, but I have to check up on the Late News.

GREG: I'm thinking about quitting my job, Sylvia.

SYLVIA: Oh?

GREG: Chucking the whole thing.

SYLVIA: What would you do instead?

GREG: Something with you, maybe.

SYLVIA: I wouldn't mind going into advertising. How would you feel about being in one of those Ralph Lauren ads in the *New York Times* Sunday Magazine? You nursing a glass of scotch, me curled comfortably on some couch. I could do that, Greg.

GREG: No, Sylvia. No advertising, please. That's even worse than trading currencies. We should do something more essential, Sylvia. Drug detection, maybe. Can you detect drugs?

SYLVIA: I'd sure like to try.

GREG: Or how about working with the blind. Or I could take you into nursing homes. Or children's wards in hospitals. Old people and kids, Sylvia. They're keyed into the essentials. They'd connect with you immediately.

SYLVIA: Hold it! (*She stops*)

GREG: What?

SYLVIA (*looking out*):   There's something there.

GREG: Where?

SYLVIA (*bending over*):   There! There! Under that parked car.

GREG: I don't see . . .

SYLVIA: Hey, hey, hey!

GREG (*seeing*):   Oh, that. That's just a cat.

SYLVIA: Knew it!

GREG: Just an old pussycat.

SYLVIA: Let me at it.

GREG (*holding her leash*):   Easy now.

SYLVIA: I said let me *at* that thing. I want to kill that fucker.

GREG (*holding her back*):   No, Sylvia. No.

SYLVIA (*to the cat*):   Hey you! Hey kitty! You're a sack of shit, you know that?

GREG: Let's move on, Sylvia.

SYLVIA: You're disgusting, kitty! You're a disgrace to the animal kingdom!

GREG: Leave it, Sylvia. Let's move along!

SYLVIA (*backing away*):   Smell that damn thing! Can you smell it? I can smell it from here! (*Coming down again*) You stink, kitty! Take a bath some time!

GREG: Now, now.

SYLVIA (*now looking at the cat upside down*):   Who are you staring at, you sneaky bastard? You staring at me?

GREG (*dragging her away*):   Let's go, Sylvia!

SYLVIA (*over her shoulder to the cat*):   Fuck you, kitty! Up yours with a ten-foot pole!

GREG: Come on now.

SYLVIA (*to the cat*):   You should be chased up a tree, you cocksucker! I'd like to bite off your tail and shove it up your ass! I hate your fucking guts, kitty, and don't you ever forget it! (*Turning to Greg; suddenly very sweetly*) Well. Out of sight, out of mind. Let's move on.

GREG: Wow, Sylvia.

SYLVIA: I'm sorry, but I had to do it.

GREG: You're full of surprises, aren't you?

SYLVIA: You want instinct, you got instinct.

GREG: I sure did.

SYLVIA: A whiff of the jungle, right? Nature, tooth and claw.

GREG: I'll say.

SYLVIA: I must say it helps to express your feelings.

GREG: I should say that stuff to Harold at work. How does it go again? You're a sack of shit, Harold! You're a disgrace to the—.

SYLVIA (*interrupting*):   Hey look! Here comes that Corgi from over on Columbus Avenue. Shall I sidle up to him or ignore him completely?

GREG: Surprise me, Sylvia. Surprise me.

(*They go off. Night. An airport waiting area. Airport music. Sounds of a jet taking off. Kate comes on in a raincoat, carrying her bag, paces, checks her watch. Blurry announcement on loudspeaker: "American Airlines Flight 203 to Indianapolis has been temporarily delayed." After a moment, Greg joins Kate*)

GREG: They said there'd be a short delay.

KATE: Damn. (*Sitting down; taking out her work*) Well, that gives me more time to prepare for the conference. You should go home, sweetie. (*She starts to work*)

GREG: I'll stick around. In case you're cancelled.

KATE: You don't have to.

GREG (*sitting beside her*): I want to.

KATE: You shouldn't even have bothered to drive me out.

GREG: I wanted to.

KATE: You wanted an excuse to skip that dinner with those clients.

GREG: I wanted to be with you.

KATE: I really should do some work.

GREG: Go ahead. I'll just sit with you.

(*Kate works for a moment*)

KATE: What about her holiness?

GREG: Who? Oh. Sylvia. What about her?

KATE: I thought she hated to be left alone.

GREG: I can't be with her every minute.

KATE: That's good to know.

GREG: She'll get me all to herself while you're gone.

KATE: Goody goody.

GREG: Besides, she has to learn to be alone occasionally. You'd think I was going to the moon the
way she looked when I left tonight. I kept saying
I'd just be gone a little while, but she gave me
this soulful look which—

KATE: All right, all right. I'm sorry I brought it up.

(*She works on her report. Greg stares off into space. The
airport music modulates into a piano accompaniment. Sylvia appears, settled comfortably on the couch*)

SYLVIA (*singing*):
   Ev'ry time we say goodbye
   I die a little.
   Ev'ry time we say goodbye
   I wonder why a little,
   Why the gods above me
   Who must be in the know
   Think so little of me
   They'd allow you to go . . .

GREG (*singing, as Kate works beside him*):
   When you're near there's such an air of spring
      about it,
   I can hear a lark somewhere begin to sing
      about it . . .
   There's no love song finer
   But how strange the change from major to
      minor
   Ev'ry time we say goodbye.

(*Loudspeaker announcement: "Flight 231 to Indianapolis is now boarding." The music continues underneath*)

KATE (*putting her work away*):   Whoops. There's my
  plane. Guess I'm off. (*Gets up; kisses him*) Goodbye, darling. See you Wednesday night.

GREG (*getting up; kissing her*):   I'll miss you.

KATE: Oh sure.

GREG: Really. I will.

(*Kate moves off, as if to get into line to board. Greg looks
after her. Music comes up*)

KATE (*singing; holding her ticket*):
  Ev'ry time we say goodbye I die a little.
  Ev'ry time we say goodbye I wonder why a
    little . . .

GREG (*singing toward Kate*):
  Why the gods above me, who must be in the
    know,
  Think so little of me, they'd allow you to
    go . . .

GREG AND KATE (*together*):
  When you're near there's such an air of spring
    about it . . .

SYLVIA (*still on the couch*):
  I can hear a lark somewhere begin to sing
    about it . . .

ALL THREE: There's no love song finer,

But how strange the change from major to
   minor . . .
Ev'ry time we say goodbye.

(*Kate goes off one way, Greg the other. Sylvia remains on the couch*)

SYLVIA (*suddenly alert*):   Hey, hey hey! (*Ultimate relief*) Knew it! It's him! He's home! (*She runs off eagerly as the music ends*)

(MUSIC: *Urban and hectic. Daytime; the apartment. Phyllis comes in. She wears a light-colored jacket*)

PHYLLIS (*looking around*):   This is lovely, Kate. I was expecting something more naive. I mean, for new arrivals. I mean, sometimes when people come to New York, they bring the provinces with them. I have a friend who moved from Tampa and brought her entire collection of sea shells. There were shells on the tables, shells on the chairs, shells everywhere you looked. I said, these shells are lovely, Sheila, but where do you shit?—I mean, sit. I mean . . . (*Kate comes on, carrying a stack of mail*) I like your apartment, Kate.

KATE (*laughing*):   Well, it's simple and convenient. (*She crosses to her desk*) Anybody here? . . . No, thank God. They must be in the park. For the umpteenth time.

PHYLLIS: Who?

KATE: Don't get me started. . . . But how lucky we ran into each other on the street, Phyllis!

PHYLLIS (*starting to take off her jacket*):   That's New York for you. The biggest small town in the world.

KATE: I'm discovering that.

PHYLLIS: Well, now you and Greg are here, Hamilton and I want to give you a small dinner party. (*Phyllis is about to toss her jacket onto the couch*)

KATE: WAIT!

PHYLLIS: What?

KATE: Not there! (*Takes the jacket*) You'll ruin that nice jacket. She leaves these great, grubby hairs. (*She carries the jacket off*)

PHYLLIS: Who?

KATE (*from off*):   Sylvia.

PHYLLIS: Sylvia?

KATE (*returning*):   The dog.

PHYLLIS: Oh. (*She checks where to sit*) You let the dog onto the couch?

KATE (*brushing off the couch*):   I do not. I absolutely forbid it. But she . . . I'd prefer not to talk about it.

PHYLLIS: Good for you. We New Yorkers all have parts of our lives we keep to ourselves. I mean, we all have private parts. I mean . . .

KATE (*laughing*):   You haven't changed since Vassar, Phyllis. . . . I hear you and Hamilton are the toast of the East Side.

PHYLLIS: Oh well. We circulate. . . . Who would you like to meet? Kitty Carlisle Hart? Charlayne Hunter Gault? Boutros Boutros-Ghali?

KATE: Anyone interested in the New York schools.

PHYLLIS: Fine. I'll organize an evening which will focus strictly on the educational—

KATE: She waits, you know. She literally waits until I'm out the door, and then she leaps onto that couch.

PHYLLIS: The dog?

KATE: Sylvia. And when she hears my key in the latch, she jumps off.

PHYLLIS: Are you sure?

KATE: I am. Once I sneaked back in, and caught her red-handed.

PHYLLIS: I hope you punished her immediately.

KATE: I tried. But she practically laughed in my face. She only listens to Greg.

PHYLLIS: Then Greg should punish her. Dogs are like children. They need to be thoroughly disciplined from the ground up.

KATE: Greg? Discipline Sylvia? Don't make me laugh.

PHYLLIS (*taking her memo book out of her purse*):   Let's talk dates for the party. Hamilton and I are booked solid . . . (*flips through pages*) . . . through October, but how about November sixth?

KATE: Fine.

PHYLLIS (*writing it in*):   Good. There are no friends like old—

KATE: I have the strong suspicion that when I'm out of the apartment, they sit on the couch *together*.

PHYLLIS: Greg and Sylvia?

KATE: They do everything together. Once I caught them sharing an ice cream cone.

PHYLLIS: How disgusting!

KATE: And she uses his hairbrush. I mean, he uses it. On her.

PHYLLIS: Hamilton has taken up goldfish.

KATE: At least they stay in their bowl.

PHYLLIS: Not necessarily.

KATE: What?

PHYLLIS: Sometimes he takes them into the bath-tub.

KATE: No!

PHYLLIS: I swear! If you bring it up, he'll deny it, but I swear I caught him at it.

KATE: Good Lord.

PHYLLIS: Look at us! Here we are talking about animals when we should be planning our party.

KATE: You're absolutely right. Let's have a drink. What would you like, Phyllis? Wine? Vodka? What?

PHYLLIS: Just fizzy water, please. I'm trying to give up alcohol.

KATE: Good for you. I'll get it. (*She goes off*)

PHYLLIS (*towards Kate offstage*):   Now fill me in on this school thing, Kate. I saw Madge MacKenzie at the Colony Club and she says you're roaming around Harlem, reciting Shakespeare.

(*Kate returns with two glasses*)

KATE: That's why I want to meet people with pull, Phyllis. I'm trying to put Shakespeare into the junior high curriculum.

PHYLLIS:　Is that possible? I mean, at that age? I mean, these days? I mean, up there?

KATE:　I hope so. If we can hook children in junior high, we might have them for life, Phyllis.

PHYLLIS:　I wish I could believe that, Kate.

KATE:　It's not just Shakespeare, Phyllis. It's language in general. These kids are fascinated by words. They rap, they rhyme, they invent these exciting phrases and metaphors just the way Shakespeare did. If we can take their energy and curiosity and imagination, and give them words, more words, good words in significant contexts, then maybe—(*Pause*) She wants to sleep in our bed, you know.

PHYLLIS:　Sylvia?

KATE:　Sylvia wants to sleep in our bed.

PHYLLIS:　You said no, I hope.

KATE:　Of course I said no. Not even outside the covers.

PHYLLIS:　I should hope not.

KATE:　But Greg fought me all the way. And continues to, on every issue. When we visited our friends the Wardwells up in Williamstown, he insisted on taking her with us.

PHYLLIS:　At least it's the country.

KATE: But it was our *anniversary,* Phyllis! How would you like to be driving through that lovely New England scenery with Sylvia drooling down the back of your neck.

PHYLLIS: I see your point.

KATE: And when we arrived, the Wardwells put us all in the same room.

PHYLLIS: You and Greg and Sylvia?

KATE: There we were, holed up together. Greg and I spent our wedding anniversary with Sylvia wandering restlessly around the room, peering over the bed and panting.

PHYLLIS: How horrible.

KATE: I mean, here I am, breaking my back trying to instill some sense of civility in American life and . . . she drinks from the john, you know.

PHYLLIS: Sylvia.

KATE: She drinks from the toilet. Sometimes, when we're trying to have a decent dinner, you can hear these great gulping sounds coming from the loo.

PHYLLIS: Good heavens.

KATE: Then she comes back in and sits slobbering by the table, eyeing us all through the meal.

PHYLLIS: You see? They're like children. They have to be exiled while we eat.

KATE: Don't I wish. (*Getting up*) But how about a refill, Phyllis?

PHYLLIS: I'm fine, thanks.

KATE: I might just shift to a little scotch. Excuse me a minute. (*She goes off*)

PHYLLIS (*towards Kate offstage*):   Now be careful, Kate. Don't start leaning on liquor. Take it from one who knows. It's the curse of our generation and it's the curse of our particular ethnic group.

KATE (*coming back in with a glass of scotch*):   He takes Sylvia out to lunch, you know.

PHYLLIS: No.

KATE: He dashes home at noon and they go out to lunch. He's found some restaurant on Amsterdam Avenue which is willing to serve Sylvia.

PHYLLIS: I'm appalled!

KATE: And lately he's been taking the afternoon off.

PHYLLIS: Hamilton sometimes does that. He sneaks down to the aquarium.

KATE: But Greg does this every day! He and Sylvia have lunch, and then they go on these long

walks. He covers the entire city. He says that with
Sylvia he meets all sorts of people, from all walks
of life. He says he's having a truly democratic
experience for the first time in his life.

PHYLLIS: I thought Greg was a Republican.

KATE: He was! He used to be.

PHYLLIS: Hamilton at least is that.

KATE: I almost wish Greg would change back.

PHYLLIS: I think all men should be Republicans,
Kate. It seems to be good for their prostate.
When Hamilton voted for Bush, why he—I can't
wait for the next election. . . . Ah, but I've been
talking too much.

KATE: I think I hate Sylvia, Phyllis.

PHYLLIS: No.

KATE: I do. I never thought I could hate anybody
—except Nixon. But now I hate Sylvia.

PHYLLIS: She's just a dog, Kate.

KATE: I don't care if she's a kangaroo. She's de-
stroying our marriage.

PHYLLIS: Oh now.

KATE: Sometimes I want to kill her, Phyllis. I want
to put D-Con in her dog dish.

PHYLLIS: Now that's a little drastic.

KATE: But I feel doomed, Phyllis. Cooped up in this small apartment with that creature.

PHYLLIS: Then draw the line, Kate. Say she's simply got to go.

KATE: I've tried. We keep making these clear agreements. But Greg keeps breaking them. Like Hitler.

PHYLLIS: Oh Kate.

KATE: I have the terrible feeling I'll be sharing my life with her for another ten years.

PHYLLIS: Do you think she'll last that long?

KATE: I know she will. But I won't. If this continues, she'll stand drooling over my grave.

(*Greg's voice is heard off*)

GREG'S VOICE: Hello!

KATE: There they are. (*Calls off*) Phyllis Cutler is here, dear! (*To Phyllis*) Now brace yourself.

(*Greg comes in*)

GREG: Here we are. . . . Why, Phyllis! Hello! Good to see you again! (*They shake hands. Sylvia rushes in*) This is Sylvia.

SYLVIA: Hello, hello, hello. (*She runs to Phyllis and immediately starts kneeing Phyllis's crotch*) Nice crotch here. Nice crotch.

PHYLLIS (*trying to protect herself*): Run along, Sylvia!

SYLVIA (*kneeing her*): This is just my way of saying hello.

KATE: Stop it, Sylvia!

GREG: Down, Sylvia!

KATE: Greg, make her stop.

GREG (*pulling Sylvia away*): DOWN, Sylvia! NO, NO.

KATE (*to Phyllis*): See what I mean?

PHYLLIS: I'm beginning to.

GREG (*to Phyllis*): She doesn't normally do that.

KATE: She does it all the *time!*

GREG: Hey listen! We've learned three new tricks today. Want to see them?

KATE: We do not.

GREG: Phyllis wants to see them, don't you, Phyllis?

PHYLLIS: Well, I—

KATE: Wait. How did you have time to teach Sylvia tricks, Greg?

GREG: I came home early.

(*Kate and Phyllis glance at each other*)

KATE: Why, Greg?

GREG: So I could teach Sylvia tricks.

KATE (*to Phyllis*):   See?

GREG: We found a quiet place in the park and practiced, didn't we, Sylvia?

SYLVIA: We did, we did.

GREG: So. First trick. Where's your little red ball, Sylvia?

SYLVIA: Huh?

GREG (*pulling the ball partly out of his pants pocket*): Find your little red ball.

SYLVIA: Oh. Gotcha. (*She goes to his pocket and takes out a little red ball. She holds it up to the others*) See? Little red ball.

GREG: Now give it to Daddy.

SYLVIA (*coyly*):   Why should I?

GREG: Give it to Daddy, Sylvia.

SYLVIA: What's in it for me?

GREG: Here's a treat if you give that ball back to Daddy, Sylvia.

SYLVIA: O.K. (*She gives him the ball*)

GREG: Good girl. (*He gives her a treat*)

SYLVIA: Thanks.

GREG: Now catch the ball, Sylvia.

SYLVIA: I'm still eating.

GREG: Catch the ball, Sylvia. (*He tosses the ball. Sylvia catches it*) Good girl!

SYLVIA (*to others*):   That was a tough one. (*She gives him back the ball*)

GREG (*hugging her*):   You are a very good girl! (*Tosses the ball offstage; Kate and Phyllis duck*) Now. Go fetch, Sylvia.

SYLVIA: Go fetch that ball?

GREG: Go fetch that ball.

SYLVIA: All right, I will. Seeing as how you're God. (*She runs off*)

KATE (*to Phyllis*):   You see what I'm up against? Notice how all conversation stops. Notice how civilization completely collapses. While we wait for Sylvia.

PHYLLIS: I might just have a small scotch, Kate.

KATE: Phyllis . . .

PHYLLIS: I want one, Kate. (*Grimly*) Right now! (*Apologetically*) Please.

(*Kate looks at her and goes off*)

GREG (*to Phyllis*):   You're worried, aren't you?

PHYLLIS: Actually, I am, Greg.

GREG: Don't be. She'll find her ball. It's probably under the hall table. (*Sylvia comes back on with the ball*) See? What did I tell you.

PHYLLIS: I am ultimately relieved.

SYLVIA: Here's the ball, Greg.

GREG (*taking it*):   Thank you, Sylvia. Good girl. Now when Kate gets back, I want you to roll over.

SYLVIA: I don't like rolling over, Greg.

GREG: I know. But I want you to do it.

(*Kate comes back with Phyllis's scotch and the bottle*)

KATE: Here you are, Phyllis.

PHYLLIS (*grabbing it*): Thank you. (*She takes a big gulp*)

KATE: Greg, I think we might put Sylvia—

GREG: Hold it. Watch this. Roll over, Sylvia.

SYLVIA (*confidingly*): This is the one I don't like, Greg.

GREG (*taking a treat out of his pocket*): Go on, Sylvia. Do it. Roll over. And you get a treat.

SYLVIA: All right. I'll do it. But I really hate this one. (*She gets down on the floor and does a reluctant and awkward roll-over*) I feel like a fool, but there you have it.

GREG: Good girl!

SYLVIA: Pay up, then.

GREG: Here you are, Sylvia. Here you are. (*To Kate and Phyllis*) See? See what we accomplished?

SYLVIA: Did you like that trick, Phyllis? (*She goes for Phyllis's crotch again*)

PHYLLIS: Go away, Sylvia!

KATE: Sylvia, stop that!

PHYLLIS: Have you tried spanking her? I don't think there's enough spanking these days. (*She takes another big gulp of her drink*)

KATE (*to Greg*):   Darling, do you think we possibly might put Sylvia in the kitchen. I mean, we want to talk to Phyllis, don't we?

GREG: Wait. Just one more trick.

(*Kate pours another drink*)

GREG (*getting out another treat*):   Speak, Sylvia.

SYLVIA: Speak?

GREG: Speak, Sylvia.

SYLVIA (*to Kate and Phyllis*):   I'm not sure what he wants here.

GREG: Speak, Sylvia. SPEAK.

SYLVIA: Now wait . . . I'm sure I know this one . . . I've just forgotten . . .

GREG: Look at this treat, Sylvia . . . you get it if you speak.

SYLVIA: It's coming back to me.

GREG: Speak, Sylvia.

SYLVIA: Hey!

GREG: Good girl.

SYLVIA: Hey! Hey!

GREG: Good girl!

SYLVIA: Hey! Hey! Hey!

GREG (*giving her the treat*): That's a very good girl, Sylvia!

SYLVIA (*chewing*): I knew I could do it.

GREG (*to Kate*): See, sweetie? She can speak!

KATE (*to Phyllis*): So much for Shakespeare.

PHYLLIS (*downing her drink*): I've got to go. (*She gets up, stumbles, recovers*)

KATE: But we've hardly talked.

PHYLLIS: I've got to be off. Really. (*Kisses her*) So nice to see you again, Kate. (*Shakes hands with Greg*) Goodbye, Greg. (*Waves at Sylvia*) Bye—bye, Sylvia.

(*Sylvia goes for Phyllis's crotch once more*)

KATE: No, Sylvia! NO!

GREG: Down, girl. (*To Phyllis*) She likes you a lot, Phyllis.

PHYLLIS: I'll tell them that at my next A.A. meeting.

(*Phyllis staggers out, quite smashed. Sylvia runs after her. We hear Phyllis's protests offstage*)

(Kate goes off, then returns angrily)

KATE: She is driving away our friends, Greg!

GREG: Oh, come on.

KATE: She is, Greg. She gave Alice Felker a bloody nose.

GREG: She thought Alice was playing.

KATE: Well, Alice wasn't. Alice was defending herself.

(Sylvia comes back on)

SYLVIA: I'd like to eat, please. Time to chow down.

KATE: Our friends loathe her.

GREG: The Wardwells loved her. They specifically said the next time we came up, be sure to bring Sylvia.

KATE: They were just being nice.

GREG: They loved her. Most people love her. People stop me in the street to pat her. Children's faces brighten as we walk by. She lightens my life.

KATE: She darkens mine, Greg.

SYLVIA: Where's dinner? I'm going to check on dinner. *(She goes out)*

GREG (*starting to follow her*):   She's hungry.

KATE (*her scotches are catching up with her*):   I want to talk about this, Greg.

GREG: We've been all through it.

KATE: We have *not* been all through it. (*She sits him down in the chair*) Did you get fired today, Greg?

GREG: What?

KATE: Did you get fired?

GREG: What makes you think that?

KATE: I have an instinct. Did you get fired?

GREG: No! Of course not. No. (*Pause*) I got temporarily laid off.

KATE: Oh Greg.

GREG: They gave me a leave of absence for medical reasons.

KATE: *Medical* reasons?

GREG: They think I need counseling.

KATE (*kneeling beside him*):   You do, darling! I really think you do!

GREG: Just because my work doesn't seem real any more.

KATE: What is real then, Greg?

GREG: Sylvia. Sylvia's real.

KATE: I'll tell you what's real, Greg. The mortgage on this apartment is real. The kids' tuitions are very, very real.

GREG: I need to feel more . . .

KATE: More what, Greg? And don't say "real."

GREG: More connected, then.

KATE: Connected . . . connected to what?

GREG: Life. (*Pause*) No. (*Pause*) Living.

KATE: I'm beginning to understand, darling.

GREG: You are?

KATE: I am, sweetie. This is another one of those things that happen to men in middle age.

GREG: No it isn't.

KATE: Yes it is, darling. I admit I'm slightly sauced, but I still know a hawk from a handsaw.

GREG: What?

KATE: It's like when poor fat old Ted Donahue tried to take up tap dancing.

GREG (*getting up*):   This is entirely different.

KATE (*getting up; slurring her words*):   Well, I'm sorry, sweetie, but whatever it is . . . (*hiking up the waistband of her skirt*) I have to say time's up.

GREG: Time's up?

KATE: Really up. I said I'd try, and I have, and it's been much longer than a few days. So I'm putting my foot down, Greg. I want you to give Sylvia away.

GREG: Away?

KATE: I want that. I am asking that. I insist upon that.

GREG: What do you mean, give her *away*? To whom?

KATE: Some farmer. Give her to some farmer.

GREG: There are no farmers any more, Kate. Farmers don't exist. Read *The New Republic*.

KATE: Oh now . . .

GREG: And I refuse to give my dog to some agricultural conglomerate. Sylvia? Being cared for by Archer-Daniels-Midland? Nope. Sorry. Can't do it.

KATE: Greg . . .

(Sylvia comes in, carrying a woman's shoe)

SYLVIA: Look what I've got!

KATE: Oh Lord, she's got my shoe.

GREG: It's a peace offering.

KATE: It is not! It's a deliberate act of aggression.

SYLVIA *(parading it around)*:   Look at this shoe! Look at this fabulous shoe!

KATE: Drop that, Sylvia! Right now!

SYLVIA: Chase me.

KATE: She'll ruin it, Greg.

SYLVIA: Chase me.

GREG: She just wants to play.

KATE *(chasing her around the couch)*:   I want that shoe, Sylvia. Immediately.

GREG: Bring it here, Sylvia. *(Sylvia finally brings the shoe to Greg; drops it at his feet)* Good girl! *(Greg picks up the shoe, brings it to Kate)* Here's your shoe, Katie.

KATE *(looking at the shoe)*:   She's ruined it.

GREG: It's an old shoe.

KATE (*on the verge of tears*):   It's my best pair! You owe me a new pair of shoes, Greg!

GREG: O.K. O.K. I'll buy you some shoes.

KATE: I'll bet she took my book, too.

GREG: What book?

KATE: My annotated copy of *All's Well That Ends Well.* I can't find it. I'll bet Sylvia took it and ate it.

GREG: She wouldn't do that.

SYLVIA: Hey! Hey! Hey!

KATE: She ate half *The New Yorker!*

GREG: It was a lousy issue anyway. *The New Yorker*'s getting—

SYLVIA: Hey, hey!

KATE: Greg, I am issuing an ultimatum.

GREG (*starting out*):   It's time for her dinner. (*To Sylvia*) Come on, sweetheart. Time to eat. (*They hurry off*)

KATE (*calling after*):   Sweetheart? Is it *sweetheart* now? Goddammit, Greg! When's the last time you said that to *me*?

(*She throws the shoe after him, then sits down hopelessly, polishing off whatever glasses of liquor are available. After a moment, Sylvia comes back on, carrying the shoe*)

SYLVIA: I believe this is yours. (*She drops the shoe at Kate's feet*)

KATE: Sylvia, I have something to say to you.

SYLVIA: What if I don't feel like listening?

KATE: Then I'll see to it that you never lick another plate.

SYLVIA (*getting onto the couch*): All right. Shoot.

KATE: Off the couch, please.

SYLVIA: Greg lets me sit here.

KATE: I don't. Off! Right now!

SYLVIA: Make me. (*Kate moves toward her*) I'm warning you! I've been known to bite!

KATE (*almost falling over onto the couch*): Try that just once, Sylvia! Just ONCE! And you are out the door! Now OFF! Right now!

SYLVIA: O.K. Cool it. I get the picture. (*She reluctantly gets off the couch*) You sure don't like me, do you?

KATE: I think it's safe to say I hate your guts.

SYLVIA: May I ask why?

KATE: Because you're messing around with my marriage.

(*Sound of Greg offstage, banging a dish*)

GREG'S VOICE: Din-din! Come and get it!

(*Sylvia starts off*)

SYLVIA: I believe I'm wanted in the kitchen.

KATE (*making a lunge for Sylvia; they both fall to the floor*): Hold it, Sylvia.

SYLVIA: Let me go!

KATE: I plan to do everything I can to get you out of here, Sylvia.

SYLVIA: I doubt if you can do very much, Kate.

(*Both are now on their hands and knees*)

KATE: Before long you're going to be cowering in some cage.

GREG'S VOICE: Dinny-poo! Sup-sup-suppertime!

SYLVIA: My master's voice, Kate.

KATE (*holding on to her*): I'm not through yet, Sylvia. Now you should know that all you are is a male menopausal moment. Oh, I know, I know, it's all been very exciting, walking around town during these fine fall days. But when winter comes, Sylvia, when it's cold in the morning and dark in the afternoon, when he has to stand shivering in the park waiting to pick up your do-do, how long do you think you'll last, Sylvia? He'll have second thoughts then, Sylvia, and I'll be right there to help him think them.

(*Sylvia struggles to get away*)

GREG'S VOICE: Sylvia! Come! Kibble time!

SYLVIA: You're forgetting one thing, Kate.

KATE: Oh. And what is that, Sylvia?

SYLVIA: He loves me.

KATE: Oh yes?

SYLVIA: He does. He thinks I shit ice cream!

KATE: There's love and there's love, sister!

SYLVIA: Yes, well, we'll see.

KATE: Yes, we'll see, Sylvia. From here on in, it's a fight to the finish.

SYLVIA: Fair enough! And may the best species win!

(They confront each other on all fours. Greg comes in, carrying a dog dish filled with kibble)

GREG *(seeing them)*: Hey! Great! Can I play, too? *(He drops to his hands and knees, next to them. Kate looks at him. Quick blackout. End of Act I.)*

Act
Two

ACT II

MUSIC: *"Autumn in New York." A suggestion of autumn foliage. Warm light. The Park. Bird sounds. Dogs yapping offstage. Greg sits on a park bench, basking in the autumn sun. Sylvia paces beside him.*

GREG: Don't you want to play with the gang?

SYLVIA: I get bored with the afternoon crowd. Nannies and babies. Schnauzers and cocker spaniels.

GREG: What you mean is, Bowser hasn't shown up yet.

SYLVIA: I mean what I mean. (*She settles beside him on the bench*)

GREG: I wish I knew more about you, Sylvia.

SYLVIA: Why do you have to know everything?

GREG: Just for the pleasure of knowing. Take Kate, for example. We started dating in high school. We know each other cold.

SYLVIA: Yeah well, that's her, this is me.

GREG: I wish I knew more about your former owner.

SYLVIA: Second owners always wish that.

GREG: Did you like him as much as you like me?

SYLVIA: How do you know it was a guy?

GREG: Good point. But you were mistreated, weren't you?

SYLVIA: I got to sleep on the couch.

GREG: Still. What kind of person would take you to the park and just let you go?

SYLVIA: How do you know I wasn't lost? Or how do you know I didn't see you sitting on a bench and simply say to myself, "There's the man I want to spend the rest of my life with." How do you know I didn't break my leash and run to your side?

GREG: I don't know, do I?

SYLVIA: And you never will. See? I'm a mystery. I'm what's known as the Other. That's never happened to you before. That's why I'm so exciting. And that's what love is all about. Now go with the flow, man. (*Louder barking and yapping offstage. Sylvia gets up and stretches*) Well. Now I think I'll just mosey on back to the group.

GREG (*looking off*): Ah. Because Bowser's there now. Right?

SYLVIA: I'm not saying a word. (*She runs off. Greg stands and watches her. Tom comes on*)

TOM: Hiya, Greg.

GREG: Hi, Tom.

TOM: How're things going at home?

GREG: Fine.

TOM: Really?

GREG: Actually, not so good.

TOM: Thought so. Think I know why.

GREG: Sylvia's why.

TOM (*sitting beside him on the bench*):   No, no. It's deeper than that. I've been reading this book.

GREG: Another book.

TOM: This one's deep, man. It's all about us.

GREG: Us?

TOM: It says we're basically biophilic.

GREG (*moving away from him on the bench*):   Hey. Watch it.

TOM: No, that's good, man. People who love dogs are biophiles. They're lovers of the *bios*—which is Greek for the processes of nature.

GREG: Go on.

TOM: What's more, the whole thing's genetic. Did your dad take you fishing and hiking when you were young?

GREG: Actually yes.

TOM: Did your mother push your stroller through some zoo?

GREG: I'm sure. Yes.

TOM: See? What they were doing was activating your biophilic gene.

GREG: I see.

TOM: We've inherited these genes from our caveman days when we had to connect with nature in order to survive in it.

GREG: Ah.

TOM: And your relationship with Sylvia has reactivated that gene. That's why you respond to her so strongly. On the other hand, your wife's biophilic gene has become thoroughly atrophied.

GREG: That's true enough.

TOM: She sees nature as threatening and messy.

GREG: You got it.

TOM: That's why you're having marital problems. It's all built in. It's as if you were straight and she was gay. Or vice versa.

GREG (*uneasily*):   I don't know, Tom . . .

TOM (*getting up*):   Look. I'm just giving you a name
   for what's going on. Naming the problem helps
   you deal with it. Actually, that's why my wife and
   I have decided to split.

GREG: Oh, I'm sorry.

TOM: No, no, it's good. Biophiles need to mate
   with other biophiles. It's better for the environ-
   ment. Bowser and I are hoping to hook up with
   a forestry major.

GREG: Good luck.

TOM: I'll lend you the book.

GREG (*getting up; looking out*):   Sylvia's having a ball
   out there.

TOM: Life of the party, isn't she?

GREG: She's been to the beauty parlor again.

(*Both watch*)

TOM: Or else she's in heat.

GREG: Naw.

TOM: She may be.

GREG: What makes you think so?

TOM: The way she carries her tush. (*They watch*) Did you ever get her spayed?

GREG: Not yet. I took your advice about waiting. (*They watch*) Is Bowser fixed?

TOM: Nope. It's different.

GREG: Is it?

(*They watch*)

TOM: Call her. See if she'll come.

GREG: Of course she'll come.

TOM: Not if she's in heat.

GREG (*calling*):   Sylvia! . . . Sylvia, come! (*To Tom*) See? She's coming immediately.

(*Sylvia comes on*)

SYLVIA: Hi, Greg! (*To Tom*) Hello, Tom. Did I ever tell you how fond I am of Bowser?

GREG: You're not in heat, are you, sweetheart?

SYLVIA: Me? Naw. No way.

GREG: Didn't think so.

SYLVIA (*to herself*):   I just feel like fucking, that's all.

TOM: She seems to be asking for it.

GREG: She's just being affectionate.

SYLVIA (*to herself*):   I want to fuckie-fuck-fuck.

TOM: I think she's definitely in heat.

GREG: It's just natural affection.

SYLVIA: May I go now?

GREG: Sure, Sylvia. Go play.

SYLVIA (*going off*):   Hey Bowser! Ready or not, here
   I come! And I want to fuck toot sweet! (*She runs
   off*)

(*Pause*)

GREG: You may be right. She may be in heat.

TOM: I think she is.

GREG: What do I do if she is?

TOM: Keep her inside.

GREG: With my *wife*?

TOM: Then send her away.

GREG: My wife?

TOM: Sylvia!

GREG: I'm not going to send her away.

TOM: Just for the duration.

GREG: Out of the question.

TOM: Then keep her on a leash at all times. And
don't bring her into the park. If you let her
loose, you're just asking for—(*looks out*) Uh–oh.

GREG: What?

TOM: Where's Bowser?

GREG: Where's Sylvia?

(*They look around*)

TOM (*finally*): Look. Over there. Behind that
bush.

(*They look*)

GREG: Shit.

TOM: I told you!

GREG (*starting off*): I'll break it up!

TOM (*holding him*): Too late. They're locked.

GREG: I don't care. I've got to—

TOM: You'd hurt her.

GREG: But . . .

TOM: Hey, Greg! Think about *her* for a change! This is her big moment! What has she done for most of her life? Lie around an apartment. Take an occasional walk at the end of a leash. Give her this, at least. Let her have something to remember.

(*They stand watching*)

GREG: That bastard.

TOM: Who? Bowser?

GREG: He raped her.

TOM: Come off it.

GREG: Bowser raped Sylvia!

TOM: She asked for it! She shoved it right in his face!

GREG (*grabbing Tom by the shirt*): Listen, fella. You're talking about my . . . (*Lets go*) Dog.

TOM: See? See what we're doing? We're thinking of them as people.

GREG: Right. (*They watch*) Oh, Sylvia . . . Sylvia . . . Sylvia . . .

TOM: After this, you should have her fixed.

GREG: And you should have Bowser neutered.

TOM: Nope. Sorry. It would ruin his personality. There's a major difference between castration and just having your tubes tied, Greg. Think about it.

GREG (*poking him in the chest*):   I see. So once again, the women of this world are being asked to suffer the consequences of male aggression. Oh boy, I'm telling you. I'm learning a lot about life these days.

TOM: Cool it, Greg.

(*They watch*)

GREG: Do these things always take?

TOM: Not always.

GREG: I almost wish it would.

TOM: Why?

GREG: Sylvia'd make a wonderful mother.

TOM: It's tough having puppies. Particularly in town.

GREG: But I'd be there for her. I'd pitch right in. I'd build a special box for her, with newspapers and a blanket, and get right in there and give a hand. It would give us more in common. Hey, when Kate and I had our kids, I pulled my weight, let me tell you. I helped feed them, and change them, and give them their baths. And on

Sunday mornings, we'd bring them into our bed and we'd all hunker down under the covers. I'd do the same with Sylvia and her pups. Why we'd all . . . together we'd . . . why, we'd . . . (*He runs out of steam. Pause*)

TOM: You're sick, man.

GREG: I know it.

TOM: Get her to the vet. First thing.

GREG (*with a sigh*): Right.

TOM: And get yourself to a shrink.

GREG: Mmmm.

TOM (*looking out*): Well. (*Watches vicariously*) Looks like they're done. (*Checks watch*) Hey. It's late . . . (*Stretches, flexes, lights a cigarette*) Come on, Bowser! Let's go, Big Guy! Shake a leg, O Studly One! (*He goes off proudly, smoking*)

GREG (*calling after him*): You macho bastard! (*Greg kicks the ground angrily. After a moment, Sylvia comes on. Pause. They look at each other*)

GREG: Well, well.

SYLVIA: You speaking to me?

GREG: Have a good time out there?

SYLVIA: I believe it's time to go home.

GREG: I said, did you have a good time?

SYLVIA: I'd prefer not to discuss it. (*Starts off*)

GREG: Do you like Bowser?

SYLVIA: Who?

GREG: You know damn well who. Bowser. That big guy with his tail up, heading home.

SYLVIA (*looking off*):   Oh, him.

GREG: Do you like him?

SYLVIA: It's really none of your business, Greg.

GREG: Oh no? Seems to me out there you made it everybody's business.

SYLVIA: Look, Greg. I happen to be exhausted.

GREG: I'll bet you are.

SYLVIA: I am tired, I am hungry, and I am not going to stand around this park discussing ancient history. What happened between me and Bowser is over and done with. It was just a fling, Greg. Just a dumb, silly fling. We both got temporarily carried away. Now let's leave it at that.

GREG: Will it happen again?

SYLVIA: What do you mean?

GREG: Are you still in heat, Sylvia?

SYLVIA (*rubbing her back against something*):   I refuse
to recognize that expression. I find it somewhat
demeaning.

GREG: You are, aren't you?

SYLVIA: I'm not saying I am, I'm not saying I'm
not.

GREG: Seems to me a little operation is in order.

SYLVIA: Which means?

GREG: Never mind, but I'm calling the vet first
thing.

SYLVIA: That sounds like you plan to punish me.

GREG: No, no.

SYLVIA: It certainly sounds that way.

GREG: It's for your own good.

SYLVIA: Oh yeah, sure. Tell me another.

GREG: I just wish you could exercise a little more
self-control.

SYLVIA: May we change the subject, please? May
we get on with our lives? (*Taking the leash, handing
him his end*) May we make some attempt to move
towards home. I happen to be quite hungry.

GREG: I'll bet you are. Let's go.

(*They start off. Suddenly she stops*)

SYLVIA: Hold it.

GREG: What?

SYLVIA (*jumping onto the bench*):   Get a load of that dalmation over there.

GREG: What about him?

SYLVIA: Look at the balls on that guy!

GREG: Let's go, Sylvia.

SYLVIA: On second thought, maybe I want to stay.

GREG (*pulling at her*):   Jesus, you're a slut, Sylvia. You're a promiscuous slut. It's under the knife for you, kid. First thing.

SYLVIA: You're jealous, aren't you?

GREG: Not at all.

SYLVIA: Yes, you are. You're jealous!

GREG: I am not! I just happen to think you can do better, that's all!

SYLVIA: Yeah, yeah, yeah . . .

(*They are off.* MUSIC: *English Renaissance: possibly Pur-cell. The apartment. Kate comes on, carrying a document. After a moment, noises are heard off*)

KATE (*trying to sound sweet*):   That you, darling?

GREG'S VOICE: Just us.

KATE: I wonder if we could talk for a minute.

(*Greg comes on*)

GREG: Sure. Sure we can talk. (*Calls off*) Come on, Sylvia.

KATE: Alone, Greg. Without Sylvia.

GREG: She'll be quiet. She's still under the weather after her operation.

(*Sylvia comes in, walking stiff-legged*)

SYLVIA: I feel like a gutted turkey.

GREG: The vet said she'll be shaky for a couple more days.

(*Sylvia stands, legs apart, looking at him resentfully*)

SYLVIA: I wish I knew what you had them do to me, you prick.

GREG (*low to Kate*):   She's a little mad at me.

KATE (*indicating her document*):   Greg, sweetheart, I have some—

GREG: Hold it, dear. . . . Lie down, Sylvia.

SYLVIA: I don't want to lie down.

GREG: Down, Sylvia. (*To Kate*) She's supposed to lie down. (*To Sylvia*) Lie *down*, Sylvia. (*Sylvia, with a sigh, slowly and carefully lies down*)

SYLVIA: Shit. That hurts.

KATE (*standing up*):   Greg, I have some very exciting—

GREG: Sit, Kate.

KATE: What?

GREG: Sit down.

KATE: Greg, I am not Sylvia.

GREG: Sorry. I got confused.

KATE: Now. Greg. I have some very exciting news. For both of us.

GREG: Shoot.

KATE (*indicating document*):   I got a grant.

GREG: You got a grant?

KATE: To study in England.

GREG: Hey!

KATE: It's from a special foundation set up for women who resume their careers after their childbearing years.

GREG (*hugging her*): Congratulations, darling! That's fantastic! It's all paying off, isn't it? Those night courses when the kids were growing up. Summer school. It's all coming together.

SYLVIA (*on the floor; groaning*):   Oooh, my gut! My aching gut!

(*Greg moves toward Sylvia, Kate tries to keep him focused*)

KATE: So I thought I'd use it to see how the English teach their mother tongue.

GREG: Great idea!

KATE: And . . .

GREG: And?

KATE (*showing him*):   They supply "a spousal supplement."

GREG: A spousal supplement?

KATE: You can come too, darling!

GREG: Fantastic!

KATE: And it couldn't happen at a better time, Greg. With your job in limbo and everything.

SYLVIA (*groaning*): Sweet Jesus, what women go through in this world!

KATE: So I thought we could get a flat in London. And maybe have the kids over for the summer.

GREG: Perfect! (*To Sylvia*) Hear that, Sylvia? Oh, to be in England! Hikes on the moors, kid! *Wuthering Heights? The Hound of the Baskervilles?*

SYLVIA (*from the floor; groaning*): Don't talk to me. I'm dying here.

GREG: Just close your eyes and think of England, Sylvia. (*To Kate*) The English are a great people. They love dogs.

KATE (*carefully*): They do, darling. They definitely do. (*Getting up*) They love them so much that they're very protective of their own.

GREG: What does that mean?

KATE: They have a quarantine, sweetheart—a six-month quarantine—before you can bring a dog into the country.

GREG: That's ridiculous.

KATE: Well, they do. I checked, darling. I called
        the consulate. Even Elizabeth Taylor's dogs were
        not allowed to set paw on English soil.

GREG: You're saying we can't take Sylvia?

KATE: I'm afraid we can't, sweetheart.

GREG: Those snooty Limey fucks!

KATE: I thought we had an agreement about that
        word, Greg.

GREG: So Sylvia isn't good enough for them, huh?

KATE: We'll just have to find her a good home,
        Greg.

(*Sylvia, on the floor, is now sleeping. She lets out a noisy
snore. Greg again moves toward her*)

KATE: Let sleeping dogs lie, Greg.

GREG (*turning to her*):   You applied for this grant,
        didn't you?

KATE: Of course I applied.

GREG: No, I mean recently. Since Sylvia.

KATE: As a matter of fact, yes.

GREG: And you specifically asked for England.

KATE: English is my field, sweetheart.

GREG: And you knew that Sylvia couldn't come.

KATE: I knew we needed to get away, Greg.

GREG: You are trying to separate me from my dog!

KATE: That's part of it, yes!

GREG: That's a major part of it!

KATE: She's not good for us, Greg! I hate what she does to you and I hate what she does to me! I think—(*she stops*) what is that awful smell?

GREG: I think it's Sylvia. The vet said she might pass a little gas.

KATE (*fanning the air*): Damnit, Sylvia!

GREG (*fanning the air*): She's had an *operation*, Kate!

KATE: Let's talk about England.

GREG: I don't want to go.

KATE: Greg.

GREG: Not without Sylvia.

KATE: If you loved me, you'd come to England!

GREG: I'll come visit.

KATE: I followed *you* around for twenty years. You can damn well follow me!

GREG: I said I'll visit!

KATE: I plan to be there for six months.

GREG: That long?

KATE: That long.

GREG: I'll last.

KATE: Maybe I *won't*, Greg.

GREG: Are you serious?

KATE: You could find her a home if you wanted to, Greg.

GREG: *This* is her home. This is *my* home.

KATE: Even without me in it?

GREG: I can't give her up, Kate. It's a genetic thing. I have this gene.

KATE: Oh, yes? Well, I have a gene, too, Greg. It's a gene that tells me I made a major commitment to my mate. It's a gene that reminds me I am responsible for educating my offspring. It's a gene that makes me want to do something constructive about the welfare of the world at large!

(Sylvia lets out another noisy snore. They both look at her)

GREG: Maybe we should sleep on this one.

KATE: Maybe we should. I'm going to bed. Are you coming?

(*Pause*)

GREG: Later.

KATE: This is serious, isn't it?

GREG: I think it is.

KATE (*to Sylvia*): Well, Sylvia, thanks a lot. You've managed to chew a huge hole in a twenty-two-year-old marriage!

(*Kate goes. Greg stands, looking after her*)

SYLVIA (*talking in her sleep, occasionally kicking*): Hey, Bowser! Wait for me, buddy!

GREG (*kneeling down beside her*): Wake up, Sylvia.

SYLVIA (*waking up*): Wumpf. What? Who? Where?

GREG: Time for your pill, kid.

SYLVIA (*getting slowly to her feet*): I hate pills.

GREG: I'll put it in with your food. You won't taste a thing.

SYLVIA: I love you, Greg.

GREG (*helping her up*): I'm a mess, Sylvia.

SYLVIA: I know you are. But even when you be-
have like a complete asshole, I love you completely.

(*They go out slowly together, Sylvia leaning on Greg.* MU-
SIC: *possibly Philip Glass. An office with a chair and desk.
Venetian blinds. Leslie, a marriage counselor, comes on
with Kate. Leslie wears a unisex outfit*)

LESLIE: I must say, Kate, I find it somewhat diffi-
cult to counsel married couples when one of the
partners refuses to cooperate. I thought your
husband agreed to join us.

KATE: He promised he would.

LESLIE: Then let's simply assume he's late.

KATE: Let's simply assume he's with Sylvia. . . .
Oh, Leslie. Maybe I should just say the hell with
the whole thing!

LESLIE: Now, now. Don't give up. We've come a
long way, you and I. Please sit, Kate.

KATE (*pacing*): I wish people would stop telling me
to sit.

LESLIE: All right, stand, then. But let's take advan-
tage of Greg's absence to review the bidding.
(*Consulting her notes*) During our last session, you
seemed to suggest that he had actually fallen in
love with Sylvia.

KATE: He has! Totally!

LESLIE: Couldn't you be exaggerating?

KATE: He says things to her that he never says to
me!

LESLIE: Such as?

KATE: "You look beautiful, you look wonderful, I
love you." All that stuff.

LESLIE: Maybe he is speaking to you *through* Sylvia,
Kate. Maybe Sylvia is simply the medium
through which he expresses his love for you.

KATE: No, this is different, Leslie. Even when we
were first married, he never looked at me the
way he looks at Sylvia.

LESLIE: And could you describe that look?

KATE: There's a sort of deep, distant light in his
eyes. A sort of . . . primeval affection.

LESLIE: Do you think . . . now how shall I put
this, Kate? . . . Do you think there is anything
physical in his relationship with Sylvia? Now be
frank.

KATE: No!

LESLIE: You're sure? These things happen. There
was a couple in here the other day who did very
peculiar things with their cat.

KATE: There is nothing physical between Greg
and Sylvia. Oh, there's a lot of patting and paw-
ing and stroking and licking—*that* goes on *ad
nauseam*. But nothing beyond that. I almost wish
there were.

LESLIE: Why do you say that, Kate?

KATE: Because then it would be just an affair. And
any wife worth her salt can deal with that! But
this! This is much deeper. I feel I'm up against
something that has gone on for hundreds of
thousands of years—ever since the first wolf
came out of the forest and hunkered down next
to the caveman by his fire.

LESLIE: But Kate, don't you think the cave*woman*
must have had ways of shooing that wolf back
into outer darkness.

KATE: I've tried! That's why I got the grant to go
to England. But all it did was aggravate the issue.
Now he loves her even more! He says nothing
becomes her like the leaving thereof. So he won't
leave her.

(*Noise off*)

LESLIE: Ah, but I believe I hear Greg.

(*Greg comes in, breathlessly*)

GREG: Sorry I'm late. (*Kisses Kate*) Hello, darling.

KATE: This is Leslie, Greg.

GREG (*shaking hands*):   Hi, Leslie. The reason I'm late is that Sylvia had to have her stitches taken out.

KATE: We're not interested, Greg.

LESLIE: No. Let him talk, Kate. You've had your say, he should have his.

GREG (*to Leslie*):   While we were at the vet's, we discovered she had worms. (*To Kate, demonstrating*) Which explains why she's been dragging her butt all over the living room rug. (*To Leslie*) But we plan to take care of that with little pink pills.

KATE (*to Leslie*):   See? See what I'm up against?

LESLIE: Kate, why don't you go in the other room and read a magazine. I'd like to talk to Greg alone, if I may.

KATE: Is there a phone out there? Maybe I'll just go ahead and reconfirm my single seat on British Airlines.

LESLIE (*ushering her out*):   No, now trust me, Kate. I've been in this business a long, long time.

KATE: But he won't listen. It's impossible to get through. (*Kate goes out*)

LESLIE: Sit down, Greg.

GREG: Thanks. (*He sits*)

LESLIE: Talk to me, Greg . . . say whatever is on your mind.

GREG: O.K. (*Pause*) She's not herself lately.

LESLIE: I'm glad you see that, Greg.

GREG: Particularly these past few weeks.

LESLIE: And why do you think that, Greg?

GREG: Oh, I know exactly why. She resents me.

LESLIE: And why do you suppose she resents you?

GREG: Because I made the decision.

LESLIE: What decision?

GREG: To have her spayed.

LESLIE: Ah . . . you're talking about . . .

GREG: Sylvia.

LESLIE: Sylvia.

GREG: You don't want me to talk about Sylvia?

LESLIE: No, I do. If you want to, Greg.

GREG: Kate doesn't like me to.

LESLIE: Well, that's Kate, Greg. As for me, I'd like very much to hear about Sylvia. Because by telling me about Sylvia, you are really telling me about yourself.

GREG: O.K. Well, to begin with, she's got great eyes.

LESLIE: Sylvia?

GREG: Sylvia. I finally understand the word "limpid" now. She's got limpid eyes. Limpid, deep, serious eyes. But that doesn't mean she's serious all the time. She laughs. I've actually seen her laugh. And she's got this great little butt. Everyone comments on her butt. When she sashays down the street, she kind of wiggles it back and forth. A lot of people stop to pat her, just because of that butt. And when we get to the park, the whole gang goes nuts for her. Even though she's been spayed, they gather around. You should see Bowser, for example—oh and hey, I found this poem that Shakespeare wrote about her.

LESLIE: Shakespeare?

GREG (*recites*):
"Who is Sylvia? What is she,
That all our swains commend her? . . ."

LESLIE: Greg.

GREG: "Holy, fair, and wise is she . . ."

LESLIE: Greg!

GREG: "The heavens such grace did—"

LESLIE: GREG!

GREG: Yes?

LESLIE: I'm afraid we're confined to the fifty-min-
ute hour.

GREG: Sorry. I get carried away.

LESLIE (*leaving the desk, standing in front of him*):
Greg, I'm going to do something here which I
normally do much farther along in the therapy
process. I'm going to put myself into the picture.

GREG: Yourself?

LESLIE: What's my name, Greg?

GREG: Kate said it was Leslie.

LESLIE: Leslie it is, Greg. Now am I a man or a
woman?

GREG: You're a . . . (*hesitates*) woman.

LESLIE: You hesitated, Greg.

GREG: Yes. Well. Sorry.

LESLIE: No, no. I wanted you to hesitate. I wanted
you to select my gender. That's why I call myself
Leslie. It's a name which works either way.

GREG: It does, doesn't it?

LESLIE: And that's why I wear these ambivalent clothes. I may be a man pretending to be a woman, or I may be a woman pretending to be a man. I let my patients select my gender, Greg.

GREG: I thought you were a woman.

LESLIE: Because you wanted me to be a woman.

GREG: I did?

LESLIE: We project our needs onto the world, Greg. Life is shapeless and absurd. We use words, names and categories to give us a sense of shape. We need that sense of shape to get through the day.

GREG: O.K.

LESLIE: You even see it in the Bible, Greg. God has Adam name the animals. So that Adam can construct his own order out of the chaos around him.

GREG: Hmmm.

LESLIE: Which brings us to your dog, Greg.

GREG: Sylvia.

LESLIE: Sylvia. You wanted your dog to be a woman, too. That's why you named her Sylvia.

GREG: She was already named Sylvia.

LESLIE: But you embraced the name. Because you needed a woman.

GREG: I already have a woman. Her name is Kate.

LESLIE (*becoming impatient*): You wanted another *kind* of woman, Greg. You wanted the subservient little wife you once kept in the suburbs. You wanted the worshipful daughter who once hung on your every word. You wanted a Sylvia, Greg. If Sylvia didn't exist, you would have had to invent her.

GREG: You may be right, Leslie.

LESLIE (*sardonically*): I think I am, Greg. (*All business*) Now these are what we therapists call "the dangerous years."

GREG: The dangerous years.

LESLIE: The years between the first hint of retirement and the first whiff of the nursing home.

GREG: Oh God.

LESLIE: No, we should make the most of these years, Greg. I, for example, am exploring the boundaries of gender identification. Kate is moving beyond childrearing to a career in the public classroom. You, on the other hand, seem to have retreated into a kind of pastoral nostalgia.

GREG: Pastoral nostalgia?

LESLIE: By acquiring Sylvia.

GREG: You think that's true?

LESLIE: I do, Greg. And I think it's time to move on. It's time for you to accept the challenges that come with later life.

GREG: Maybe so.

LESLIE: Drop the leash, Greg, and once again take hold of your wife's hand. See if you are capable of walking with her, side by side, toward the setting sun.

GREG: Thank you, Leslie. This all makes a lot of sense.

LESLIE: I think it does, Greg. I think it makes a great deal of sense. (*Gets up, stretches*) I must say I'm exhausted. This has been a long, tough haul for all of us. (*Smiles*) Well. Now may I bring in Kate so we can all sit down together and work through a few specifics.

GREG: Aren't you forgetting one thing?

LESLIE: What thing, Greg.

GREG: Sylvia.

LESLIE: Sylvia?

GREG: You've seen Kate, you've seen me, don't you think you should see Sylvia?

LESLIE: You want me to hold a session with your dog?

GREG: Not a *session*, Leslie! Jesus, what kind of a nut case do you think I am? No, I just think you should pat her, maybe play with her a little, possibly take her for a short walk. Because then you'll see, Leslie . . .

LESLIE: See what?

GREG: Then you'll see that Sylvia is more than just a name, or a gene, or a psychological symptom or anything else that tries to pin her down. Any dog owner knows this. If you don't, Leslie, you should get one immediately. We should all have dogs. It should be put in the constitution. It's not just a right, it's an obligation. When you register to vote, you pick up your dog license. The world would be a far better place, Leslie. Why just think: you and I and Nelson Mandela and Yassir Arafat and Meryl Streep could all meet at Club Med or someplace, and what would we talk about? Our dogs, Leslie! Our dogs.

(*Long pause*)

LESLIE (*quietly*): Greg.

GREG: Yes?

LESLIE: Greg, I'd like you to leave right now. Quickly, if you would. And send Kate in on your way out.

GREG (*looking at watch*): It's Sylvia's dinner time, anyway. (*Hurries out, as Kate comes back in*)

KATE: What hap—

LESLIE: Kate: I want you to do several things.

KATE: Several . . . ?

LESLIE: First, I want you to divorce Greg.

KATE: Divorce—?

LESLIE: Take him for every nickel he's got!

KATE: Oh, I couldn't—

LESLIE: Then I want you to get a gun.

KATE: A gun?

LESLIE: To shoot Sylvia. I hope you get her right between the eyes.

KATE: But . . .

LESLIE: Sorry. I'm late for my shrink. (*Exits quickly, tearing up the case folder*)

KATE (*remaining; to herself*): "If this were played on the stage now I would condemn it as an improbable fiction." *Twelfth Night.* Act III.

(*She exits.* MUSIC: *possibly Vera Lynn singing "Now is the Hour." The apartment. Greg enters with Sylvia. She is now wearing a very attractive little black dress*)

GREG (*taking the leash out of her hand*): You look particularly glamorous today, Sylvia.

SYLVIA: Thank you, Greg.

GREG: You know why, don't you?

SYLVIA: Tell me, while I check out *le* kibble *du jour.* (*She goes off*)

GREG (*calling after her*): You look particularly glamorous because we've come to a major moment in our relationship.

SYLVIA (*returning*): A major moment?

GREG: A turning point. And at turning points in our lives, good or bad, we instinctively shine. Our eyes sparkle, our hair glistens, our bodies seem to know.

SYLVIA: But why is this a turning point?

GREG: We're going to lay our cards on the table. Both of us.

SYLVIA: I thought we always did that anyway.

GREG: We did. We do. But this will be even more so. Up until now, you've been saying what I hoped you'd say. This time, I want you to feel you're totally on your own.

SYLVIA: Sounds exciting.

GREG: Would you like to sit down, Sylvia.

SYLVIA (*slyly*):   Where shall I sit?

GREG: Anywhere you want.

SYLVIA: Can I sit on the couch?

GREG: You may, Sylvia. Come on. I'll even give you a hand. (*He helps her onto the couch*)

SYLVIA (*making a big deal of it*):   Dis is da life! I like these major moments, Greg.

GREG: Sylvia: I have to send you away.

SYLVIA: Away?

GREG: To somewhere else.

SYLVIA: Oh, you mean that kennel you put me in when you went off on that weekend? I can live with that. As long as it's just a few days.

GREG: It's not a kennel, Sylvia. I've found a family for you.

SYLVIA: Fine. Sounds better than a kennel.

GREG: And it won't be for just a few days.

SYLVIA: How long will it be? Two weeks? Three?

GREG: Forever, Sylvia.

SYLVIA: Forever?

GREG: It boils down to you or Kate, Sylvia. And I'm choosing Kate.

SYLVIA: You're choosing *Kate?*

GREG: I have to, Sylvia.

SYLVIA: You can't have us both?

GREG: I guess I can't.

SYLVIA (*leaving the couch*):   Is this because she hates me?

GREG: She doesn't *hate* you, Sylvia.

SYLVIA: She sure doesn't like me.

GREG: She doesn't like *me*, Sylvia. When I'm with you.

SYLVIA: Lord knows, I've tried to please her.

GREG: You have, Sylvia.

SYLVIA: I always greet her when she comes home.

GREG: I know that.

SYLVIA: She seems to like it when I lick the plates before they go in the dishwasher. She even encourages the habit.

GREG: That's only because she doesn't like waste, Sylvia.

SYLVIA: So you're choosing her over me.

GREG: She's my wife, Sylvia. She's the mother of my children. We've lived together a long, long time.

SYLVIA: Do you love her?

GREG: I do. Very much.

SYLVIA: I thought you loved me.

GREG: I do, sweetheart. But in a different way. And it's not a good way, as far as Kate is concerned.

SYLVIA: I thought there was talk of you and me moving out.

GREG: There was.

SYLVIA: I thought there was serious talk of you and me getting a studio apartment over on 69th Street, right near the park.

GREG: There was talk of that, yes, Sylvia. In the heat of the moment.

SYLVIA: I thought we were going to take a camping trip on Chesapeake Bay. I thought you were going to teach me to retrieve ducks.

GREG: I was going to do all that, Sylvia.

SYLVIA: And you've suddenly chickened out?

GREG: That's what I've done. Chickened out.

(*Pause*)

SYLVIA: I feel awful.

GREG: So do I.

SYLVIA: Know what I wish I could do? Mix myself a double Absolut vodka on the rocks with a twist.

GREG: I did that earlier, Sylvia. For myself.

SYLVIA: Yeah, well, being a dog, I don't happen to have the solace of alcohol, Greg.

GREG (*reaching into his jacket pocket*): I've got a Bark Bar for you.

SYLVIA: A what?

GREG: A Bark Bar. Remember? I bought you one on our last walk over to the East Side. You loved it. (*He holds it out*)

SYLVIA (*taking it, looking it over*):   It's in the shape of a cat.

GREG: I thought you'd be amused by that.

SYLVIA: Amused? Amused by those fuckers? (*Takes a bite*) Not bad. (*Chews*) But not good enough. (*Sits in the chair*) Tell me about this family you're shipping me off to.

GREG (*kneeling beside her*):   They're great, Sylvia. I advertised in the Westchester newspapers. I interviewed a number of applicants.

SYLVIA: Thanks for letting me in on it.

GREG: You'll be living in the suburbs, Sylvia.

SYLVIA: I hate the suburbs.

GREG: What? All that green grass? This family has half an acre, all fenced in.

SYLVIA: That Akita in the park used to live in the suburbs. He said you're totally alone out there. There's no sense of being part of a pack. And if you try to meet someone by taking a walk, there's a good chance you'll get run over.

GREG: You won't want to take walks, Sylvia. You'll want to stay close to home.

SYLVIA: Why?

GREG: Because you'll like this family so much.

SYLVIA: Why?

GREG: Well, for one thing, they have children.

SYLVIA: How many?

GREG: Three.

SYLVIA: Any babies?

GREG: One.

SYLVIA: I hate babies.

GREG: You don't, Sylvia. You're always licking their faces.

SYLVIA: Their mouths taste good, but they're always stepping on your tail.

GREG: Well, there are also two teenagers, Sylvia. They're eager to have you. They want to teach you to play Frisbee. They want to take you to Little League games. They'll be much better for you than I could possibly be.

SYLVIA: I hate teenagers.

GREG: You don't.

SYLVIA (*getting up*): I do. I hate them. They're totally unreliable. They forget to feed you. They play music which hurts your ears. One minute they're showering you with love, then they leave you locked in some car for hours on end—(*throw-*

ing herself on him) oh, Greg, don't do this to me! Please! Don't send me away! Keep me here with you! Please!

GREG: I can't.

SYLVIA: I'll change, Greg. I'll change my ways. I'll stop chewing shoes. I'll bring Kate *The New York Times* every morning—well I won't do that, that's too corny—but I'll do something else! Just tell me what to do, and I'll do it!

GREG: I promised Kate I'd give you away, Sylvia. I made that promise. To my wife.

SYLVIA: When?

GREG: Today.

SYLVIA: To*day*?

GREG: I'm driving you out right now.

SYLVIA: Can't I even say goodbye to Bowser?

GREG: You just saw him in the park.

SYLVIA: Jesus, you're something, Greg. You really are. You bring me home, you get me all dependent on you, you spay me . . .

GREG: Sylvia . . .

SYLVIA: You had me *spayed,* Greg! You destroyed my womanhood. And then, when I get over that, when I still decide that the sun rises and sets only in your direction, then suddenly you're packing me off to some boring nuclear family in West-chester County. Christ, Greg! Don't you feel guilty about this?

GREG: I do, Sylvia. I feel terrible.

SYLVIA: I mean, shit. You have a moral obligation here! What would the Humane Society say about this? How would they react at the S.P.C.A.?

GREG: They'd say I'm doing the right thing!

SYLVIA: Bullshit! That's just bullshit, Greg!

GREG: They'd say that a week out there with your new family and you'll forget all about me.

SYLVIA: Never!

GREG: Sure you will. If I came out to visit you, you might run up for a pat and a sniff, but that would be that.

SYLVIA: You're so wrong, Greg! You're so god-damn wrong! Read the *Odyssey* some time. That guy was gone for twenty years and when he fi-nally got home, the first person to recognize him —before his nurse, before his son, before his own *wife*, goddamnit—was his dog! That dog was ly-ing outside the palace for all those years, waiting for him, Greg. Lying on a dung heap just waiting for his master. And when his master finally showed, what did the dog do? He raised his head, wagged his tail and died.

GREG (*hugging her*):   Oh, don't, Sylvia!

SYLVIA: I'll never forget you, Greg! Ever!

GREG: Stop, Sylvia! Please! I can't stand this.

SYLVIA: Well. (*She finishes her biscuit*) Let's get it over with. (*She gets up, takes his arm à la Blanche Dubois*) I'll have to depend on the kindness of strangers. . . . Take me to the suburbs. I hope I can at least sit next to you on the front seat. After all, her majesty won't be there to object.

(*Kate's voice is heard from offstage*)

KATE'S VOICE: Hello!

SYLVIA: Or will she?

GREG: What's she doing home?

SYLVIA: Christ! I feel like sneaking off and hiding under some bed! (*She goes off*)

(*Kate comes on*)

GREG: I thought you had a meeting.

KATE: It broke up early.

GREG: We're just getting ready to go.

KATE: Where's Saliva?

GREG: Sylvia, Kate.

KATE: Where is she?

GREG: At the moment, I imagine she's trying to stay out of your hair. (*Starts off*)

KATE: Greg.

GREG: What?

KATE: I know this is hard for you.

GREG: Damn right.

KATE: I want you to know I appreciate it.

GREG: Thanks.

KATE: We'll have a good time in England, Greg. It will be a whole new thing.

GREG: I can't talk about it, Kate. It's too painful at the moment. (*Starts off again*)

KATE: Do you plan to take all her stuff?

GREG: They're in a bag in the front hall.

KATE: Her bed? Her brush? Her kibble dish?

GREG: They're all there.

KATE: What about her little red ball?

GREG: I can't find it.

KATE (*looking under a couch pillow*):   She liked that little red ball.

GREG: At least you noticed.

KATE: It's a shame to send her off without it.

GREG: She'll survive. (*He starts off again*)

KATE: Actually, my meeting is still going on, Greg. I ducked out early.

GREG: Oh, yes?

KATE: I thought I should come home and say goodbye.

GREG (*sarcastically*):   To Saliva?

KATE: To Sylvia.

GREG: Why?

KATE: I wanted to.

GREG: Magnanimous in victory, eh?

KATE: Greg . . .

GREG: Well. Have your farewell scene. (*Calls*) Sylvia! Come! (*Pause*) I don't think she wants to. (*Calls again*) Sylvia!

(*Sylvia comes on reluctantly, now dressed in the scruffy outfit she was first found in*)

SYLVIA (*sarcastically*):   You called, massa?

GREG: Kate wants to say goodbye to you.

SYLVIA: Oh, sure. And I'm Marie of Rumania. (*Starts off again*)

KATE: Come here, Sylvia.

SYLVIA (*to Greg*):   Who's she kidding?

KATE (*holding out her arms*):   Sylvia. Come.

GREG: Go on, Sylvia. She's human. Say goodbye.

(*Sylvia crosses warily to Kate. Kate embraces her while Sylvia stands stiffly*)

KATE: Sylvia, I know it's been tough sledding between you and me, but I do want to say goodbye.

SYLVIA (*over her shoulder to Greg*):   What is this? Some sudden sisterhood thing?

GREG: Easy now.

KATE: I wish . . . I wish it could have been otherwise, Sylvia.

SYLVIA (*breaking away*):   So do I, and now can I go?
(*She goes to Greg*)

GREG: We'll be off then, Kate.

KATE: Goodbye, Sylvia.

SYLVIA (*over her shoulder*):   Yeah, yeah.

(*Sylvia and Greg go out*)

KATE (*standing, calling after them*):   Greg, you should
at least stop at the pet store, and get her another
little red—

(*Sylvia comes back on, carrying a paperback. She drops it
at Kate's feet*)

SYLVIA: I hear you've been looking for this.

KATE (*picking it up*):   My *All's Well That Ends Well!*

SYLVIA: Whatever.

KATE (*looking it over*):   And it's in reasonably good
shape, Sylvia. There's just one little chew mark
here on the corner.

SYLVIA (*singing defiantly à la Piaf*):   *Rien de rien . . .
Je ne regrette rien . . .*

(*Greg comes back on*)

GREG: She found it in the hall closet and insisted
on bringing it right in.

KATE: *You* found it, Greg. And sent her in with it.

GREG: Suit yourself, Kate . . . I'll call the garage. (*He goes out*)

SYLVIA (*over her shoulder to Greg*):   I'll be right with you.

GREG (*as he goes*):   O.K.

SYLVIA (*to Kate*):   I've been thinking about what you said.

KATE: What I said?

SYLVIA: "I wish it could have been otherwise." I've been thinking about that. Know what "otherwise" is, Kate? Otherwise is that man who ran off with his grandchildren's *au pair*. Or that guy who took a shot at his wife while she was doing her step aerobics. Otherwise is those sad couples sitting in restaurants night after night, eyeing each other, with absolutely nothing to say. That's otherwise, Kate.

KATE: Is it, Sylvia?

SYLVIA: Yes, and I'll tell you what this–wise is. This–wise is the fact that he can never be happy with me unless you like me, too. Which is why he is always foisting me on you. Which is called sharing, Kate. Which is what some people sometimes call love. That's this–wise, Kate.

GREG'S VOICE (*from off*):   O.K., Sylvia. Let's go.

SYLVIA: Of course what do I know? I'm only a dog.

(*She goes off. The sound of a door closing offstage. Kate looks after them. Music begins softly underneath, the majestic, slowly-building* tuba mirum *section of the* Dies Irae *from Verdi's* Requiem. *Kate stands and thinks. Then she goes and sits in the chair; begins to thumb through her book. Something makes her uncomfortable. The music builds. She shifts her position. She reaches under the cushion, retrieves Sylvia's little red ball. She clasps it, then holds it aloft triumphantly while the music begins to come to a climax. She rises majestically, strides to the doorway as the music reaches its crescendo, then stops. A moment*)

KATE (*to herself*):   Oh, hell. As Shakespeare once said, "What the fuck."

(*She goes off determinedly after Greg and Sylvia. Greg comes on quickly from the opposite side as the lights focus on him*)

GREG (*to audience*):   We never got to the suburbs. I called and said we'd changed our minds. The folks understood, of course. Being dog lovers like ourselves.

(*Kate comes back on*)

KATE (*to audience*):   And I changed my mind about England. Oh I went—for a few weeks. But for the most part, I stayed here. While Greg looked around for another job.

GREG (*to audience*): And Sylvia stayed. She stayed with us for the next eleven years, until every-thing went wrong with her and we had to put her down. I held her when the vet gave her the shot. She looked at me, gave a little sigh, lay down quietly and died. (*Pause*) Kate was waiting for me when I got home, and we both cried.

KATE (*to audience*): That's not true. I did not cry.

GREG: You did. You just won't admit it.

KATE (*to audience*): Sylvia and I never really liked each other. Even later on.

GREG: You got along famously.

KATE (*to audience*): We tolerated each other. If that.

GREG (*to audience*): Once I came home from my new job with Wildlife Conservation International . . . and found Kate and Sylvia side by side on the couch.

KATE (*to audience*): This is an absolute lie!

GREG (*to audience*): Kate was reading *The Hidden Life of Dogs* and Sylvia had her head in Kate's lap.

KATE (*to audience*): This is a total male fantasy!

GREG (*to audience*): I'll also tell you something else. Over the years a strange thing happened. Sylvia and I didn't talk so much.

KATE (*to audience*):   Now this *is* true.

GREG: Oh, we *talked*. But less and less. It was as if we learned to understand each other *without* talking. Or maybe we learned that we could never understand each other.

KATE (*coming close to him, taking his arm*):   Or maybe it was because you and I talked more.

GREG: Whatever. (*To audience*) But Sylvia's looks changed, too.

KATE (*to audience*):   They did. She began to look . . . well, different. (*To Greg*) Show them the picture.

GREG (*to audience*):   I'll show you Sylvia's picture. (*He takes out his wallet, opens it, displays a small color photograph. Behind, we see a large, appealing blown-up photograph of an ordinary dog*) There. That's Sylvia.

KATE (*to audience*):   I took that picture the year before she died.

GREG (*to audience*):   Note who took it.

KATE (*to Greg, as they look at their picture*):   I'm afraid she looks a little the worse for wear.

GREG: She does not, Kate! She still looks absolutely gorgeous! (*Affectionately*) Ah, Sylvia!

KATE (*with a sigh*):   Oh, Sylvia.

(The lights fade on Greg and Kate, very much together, looking at Sylvia's picture. Behind them, the large photo of Sylvia stays lit a little longer. Music comes up, possibly the Benny Goodman Quartet rendition of "Ev'ry Time We Say Goodbye.")

THE END